What
STOPPING
Me from Getting
AHEAD?

Library of Congress Cataloging-in-Publication Data

Goldfarb, Robert W.
    What's stopping me from getting ahead? : what your manager won't tell you
about what it really takes to be successful / Robert W. Goldfarb.
        p.   cm.
    Includes index.
    ISBN 978-0-07-174126-2
    1. Success in business.   2. Professional employees—United States.
3. Work environment—United States.   4. Interpersonal communication.
5. Career development.   I. Title.

HF5386.G5844   2010
650.1—dc22   2009052618

1 2 3 4 5 6 7 8 9 10 11 12 13 14 15 16   DOC/DOC   1 9 8 7 6 5 4 3 2 1 0

ISBN 978-0-07-174126-2
MHID   0-07-174126-7

Interior design by THINK Book Works

McGraw-Hill books are available at special quantity discounts to use as premiums and
sales promotions or for use in corporate training programs. To contact a representative,
please e-mail us at bulksales@mcgraw-hill.com.

This publication is designed to provide accurate and authoritative information in regard
to the subject matter covered. It is sold with the understanding that the publisher is not
engaged in rendering legal, accounting, or other professional services. If legal advice
or other expert assistance is required, the services of a competent professional person
should be sought.

—*From a Declaration of Principles Jointly Adopted by a Committee of the American Bar
Association and a Committee of Publishers and Associations*

What's
STOPPING
Me from Getting
AHEAD?

What Your Manager
Won't Tell You About
WHAT IT REALLY TAKES
TO BE SUCCESSFUL

ROBERT W. GOLDFARB

New York   Chicago   San Francisco   Lisbon   London   Madrid   Mexico City
Milan   New Delhi   San Juan   Seoul   Singapore   Sydney   Toronto

To Muriel and to Kevin, Leda, Steve,
Shanna, Jeff, Kim, Jesse, Cara,
Sam, and Isaac, with love

CONTENTS

ACKNOWLEDGMENTS

Without the enduring support of my wife, Muriel, this book would have remained an idea. Without Tom Donohue and Mark French, it would not have found a publisher. Without Leah Spiro, John Aherne, and Charles Fisher, it would not have been published.

I also owe my gratitude to those who mentored me, to the leaders who entrusted their employees to my mentoring, and to the men and women on five continents who trusted me with their careers. This is your book, too.

INTRODUCTION

You try to smile as you congratulate the person just promoted to the job you worked so hard to win—the job you considered yours. How could this happen? Is management blind? Don't they see you are smarter, have been here longer, achieve more, work harder, and have more experience? You know that weeks from now you'll be sleeplessly wondering "Why not me?"

While advising and coaching more than eight hundred managers from CEO to junior buyer on five continents in more than sixty public and private corporations, nonprofit organizations, law firms, and government agencies, I've endlessly peeled back the onion to reach the core of why some employees are promoted while others—often far more qualified—are bypassed or fired.

At the onion's core are the reasons for denying promotion or firing someone you'd hear only in a senior manager's most unguarded moments. Shake that manager awake at 3 A.M. and he or she would utter judgments that seem too minor, too personal to doom a career: "He's always five minutes late to meetings." "She's on her Black-Berry when she should be listening." "He's arrogant and gives credit to no one but himself." "She's always the first to speak and interrupts when others are talking." "He dismisses ideas from other employees, claiming they won't work." "He says he's laid-back; I say he doesn't care." "She's always telling us how great her former company was." "He never confronts you directly, always complaining to someone else." "She rolls her eyes or deliberately stares at her watch when she disagrees." "He overwhelms you with details."

Few senior managers would ever publicly admit these reasons for bypassing or firing someone, instead substituting faults commonly found in a performance review: "His results could have been better." "She was slow to implement new systems." "The factory looked sloppy." "She's not motivating her sales associates." "He isn't adding value." "She's made too many bad hires." "He doesn't spend enough time in the field." "I'm not getting fresh ideas from her." "He's not thinking strategically enough." But these are comments expected in a performance review, not the real reason the boss decided "I don't want that person on my team."

On late shifts, during red-eye flights, and at restaurants about to close, senior managers confide to me why they are denying a promotion or firing someone—reasons far less politically correct than these managers would admit publicly.

The London investment banker in his somber office and the Louisiana paper mill superintendent shouting to be heard would be startled to learn they find the same behavior unacceptable. They, and others across the world with little in common except the power to end careers, speak the same words when saying no to a promotion or yes to a termination.

Behind virtually every decision I've ever heard for bypassing or dismissing an employee are twelve characteristics common to every workplace, every language. In their most private moments, managers cite one or more of these twelve reasons when they tell me, "I don't want an employee if he or she":

Lacks Integrity Lacks integrity, manipulates, claims credit for the work of others, or causes me to mistrust him or her

 Overlooks What's Important Overlooks what's important to me, never wondering "Is this what my boss wants?"

 Selfish Seeks personal credit and resents working with others toward a common goal

 Arrogant and Dismissive Is arrogant and dismissive, provoking opposition from associates, even when he or she is right

 Refuses to Yield Refuses to yield on even the smallest point, placing ego above the organization

 Rigidly Analytical Is rigidly analytical, having little patience for intuition or "gut feel"

 Old Boys' Club Mentality Discounts those of different gender, race, or ethnicity

 Lacks Passion for Change Lacks passion for change, seeing fresh ideas as impractical

 Can't Manage Former Peers Is uncomfortable managing former peers, seeking their friendship rather than their respect

Doesn't Delegate Doesn't delegate, finding it easier to just do it than to hold others accountable

Focuses on problems rather than solutions, always warning that "the sky is falling"

Uses humor as a weapon, causing coworkers to wonder "If that's supposed to be funny why does it hurt?"

You might argue, "So what if my behavior isn't like everyone else's? I get the job done." Your boss also wants the job done; you're being paid to hit objectives, to make things happen. But your boss will not allow your actions or attitude to fracture the organization. Your boss expects you to attain—even surpass—the objectives set for you without leaving wreckage behind.

Those objectives are highly quantitative: revenues, market share, products made or sold, gross margins, patients treated, funds raised, patrons served, premium income earned, houses built, clients won, budgets met. But of equal or even greater importance to senior managers—at the onion's core—are the emotions you arouse in hitting those objectives.

Bosses who grudgingly excuse a questionable decision will not tolerate questionable behavior. They've stumbled on the way up and know you will too. Even the most demanding will concede that you'll be fine so long as you learn from your mistakes and don't keep making them.

But bosses are far less forgiving when you embarrass them, are rudely combative, speak disdainfully of the enterprise, waste time, shirk accountability for errors, show contempt for associates or customers, are arrogant, mistreat subordinates, or are passive rather than passionate about your job—traits that define you more as a human being than as an employee.

There is a balance in every relationship, personal and professional. Your performance, knowledge, seniority, and experience weigh heavily in that balance. An attitude that offends associates as well as behavior contrary to the culture of the organization are also placed on that balance. If a series of personal missteps begins to outweigh your strengths, you will tip the balance and find yourself judged "not right for the job."

Executives throughout the world look first at your performance; it can be evaluated objectively in all languages. But in every workplace, on every continent, I see those executives put data aside and look inward before approving a promotion or contemplating a termination, asking themselves, "Are you the right person for this job, this organization?"

You wouldn't have been hired if you couldn't do the job. Your track record, vision, and potential have made you a candidate for promotion. But as you ascend or revenues shrink, you attract increasing attention from those above you. Here perceptions become more important than comments on a performance review. A history of "Exceeds Expectations" means little if a more demanding audience begins to question your attitude, behavior, or character.

Senior managers watch closely to determine if you're ready for broader responsibility or if you have become expendable in a harsh economy. What they are assessing is how you get the job done through an expanding constellation of people. Your behavior and attitude, as much or more than specific skills, are shaping that assessment—

and your future. As competitors from countries with exotic names become a force in the marketplace, your ability to build relationships across cultures and time zones is also being evaluated.

The gifted genius whose arrogance has previously been tolerated will tip the balance when abrasiveness outweighs value. Even in the most profit-obsessed investment banking firm, your numbers can be eclipsed by behavior deemed unacceptable. Soft virtues eventually trump hard skills.

Every successful enterprise—public, private, and nonprofit—is thinning ranks. Fewer people are doing more work. Employees are expected to absorb new responsibilities rapidly and with little training.

You must run while learning to walk. Quarterly reports loom relentlessly, and patience in the executive suite is thin. Judgments on potential are made quickly, often with little evidence. One or two questionable acts can prove lethal to your career. Older staff members are retired earlier and are no longer there to pull you aside for friendly advice.

Human Resources managers do their best to remove emotion from the decisions that get people promoted or fired, urging managers to "ladder" their employees, ranking them from marginal to outstanding. Done when an organization is thriving, such rankings are dispassionate; it's clear who has exceeded expectations through the years and who has barely met them.

But, in most organizations I go to, "laddering" is easily put off while income is surging. When managers do meet to assess their employees, discussions are rambling, interest wanes, and an air of "We're making money, so why are we doing this?" wafts into the room.

The first serious evaluations often don't take place until revenues begin to decline. Suddenly names are called for and outplacement lists compiled. You might have exceeded expectations for years, but your boss's anxiety and the need to make cuts immediately bring your most recent actions into sharp relief. The successes you achieved two years ago will not keep your name from that "hit" list if your boss feels he or she spends more time thinking about your current behavior than your past performance. Senior managers have little tolerance for employees whose actions add stress to an already demanding workplace.

What's Stopping Me from Getting Ahead? contains everything I have learned during three decades about how to avoid behavior that stamps you as "not the kind of person we want in this job or in this organization." I wrote this book because it wounds me to see promising careers sidetracked—perhaps permanently—by behavior and attitudes that offend others. Too often I've seen small missteps end potentially big careers.

More than 85 percent of the managers I work with have ceased behaving in ways that previously doomed them to lesser jobs. They acknowledged that behavior which defined them was not working. Tired of being passed over or fired, they committed themselves to erasing perceptions their actions and attitudes had created. They made enduring changes in their behavior and have moved to higher levels of management, fulfilling their potential.

The 15 percent I fail to reach share common characteristics: they blame "politics" for their inability to advance;

they point fingers at others, never themselves; they are contemptuous of rules, written and unwritten; they see themselves as victims of an inflexible organization; they blame the job, rejecting any hint that their behavior is at fault; or they see associates as the problem and defy *them* to change. When they leave the organization, they carry these same traits to their new jobs.

The hundreds of interviews I have conducted with managers whose careers have stalled and their bosses reveal how differently the two can see the same behavior. One is convinced his or her behavior is perfectly acceptable. The other finds it so unacceptable that a career is at risk.

This book describes that behavior and how to avoid it through case studies taken directly from today's workplace. These case studies will examine each of the twelve characteristics common to failing careers.

Each case study will describe how you might behave in varying situations and how you and your boss can view that behavior differently. That difference can make or break your career.

Next, I'll step between you and your boss to describe how I—an objective outsider—see that same situation.

Finally, I'll suggest specific actions you can take to win your boss's approval when you are considered for promotion.

Each case study will look like this:

- What You See
- What Your Boss Sees
- My Diagnosis
- Actions I Recommend

PART 1

Behavior Your Boss Will Not Tolerate

The faces of senior managers clench in frustration when they tell me about employees who ignore what is significant to them. "I expect my managers to know what's important to me. It's a very short list, and I repeat it often enough. Business is down sharply, and a major mistake could damage this company irreparably. It's those mistakes I worry about. So, when someone ignores what's important to me, they're putting the enterprise at risk. I'll forgive errors anyone can make but will not tolerate behavior that harms this company and its people."

The following case studies describe such behavior and how to avoid it.

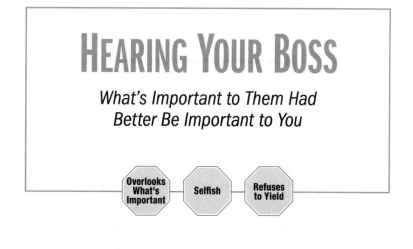

HEARING YOUR BOSS

*What's Important to Them Had
Better Be Important to You*

Overlooks What's Important — Selfish — Refuses to Yield

What You See

Suzanne C., Machine Tool Designer, manufacturing company

I design complex tools and dies and get the job done as well or better than my male associates. But my boss always finds fault with things that have nothing to do with my job performance. Our manufacturing managers are old school and roll their eyes if you're two minutes late, but they'll waste time talking about last night's football game. Good grief, I once brought coffee and a muffin to a morning meeting and my boss glared at me! He doesn't see that I turn out more original work in a week than others do in a month. They're intimidated by outdated software while I design tooling that increases machine output by 20 percent. Why worry about muffins when I save the company time and money?

What Your Boss Sees

Tom R., Vice President, Technical Services

Suzanne is bright, quick, and current with new technology. But she's oblivious to what's important around here: being on time, treating work as serious, and showing operating divisions we're as committed to the business as they are. She doesn't realize people here—especially old-timers—bleed for this company. They have little tolerance for someone who seems cavalier. I've won the trust of our factory people because they know I consider technology just another tool that serves manufacturing. But they'll quickly judge us as impractical nerds if Suzanne waltzes into meetings late and with a picnic lunch. I've got a big problem—how to tell her she's not ready for promotion and may even be putting her job at risk.

MY DIAGNOSIS

Most bosses are quick to define their expectations of you, providing detailed objectives and deadlines. While fluent in data, many are uncomfortable confronting something as unquantifiable as attitude and questionable behavior. Bosses are less likely to discuss what they consider "soft issues," saying, "Why do I have to tell her? She should know better." Tom has spent years winning the confidence of factory supervisors suspicious of new technology, and he doesn't want Suzanne to jeopardize that trust.

Suzanne has two problems; she doesn't realize that what's trivial to her is very important to her boss, and he hasn't told her that's a problem. Like so many women, she works for a man who is reluctant to criticize her. While the glass ceiling has risen and women are entering careers once closed to them (until very recently the only women in Suzanne's machine shop were on calendars), many men fear they will be accused of sexual harassment if they criticize a woman as they would a man. Other men are simply uncomfortable managing women and say little to avoid any unpleasantness.

Men like Tom hope female employees will decipher oblique hints and change their behavior. Male subordinates can also suffer from this lack of directness but generally have an informal network to tell them where they're going wrong.

If Suzanne developed her own informal network, this is what she would probably hear:

ACTIONS I RECOMMEND

1. Listen to not only what your boss says but to what you sense your boss is *not* saying. Do you sense he is holding back, reluctant to say something that might upset you? You can decipher the unspoken by being alert to casual, seemingly irrelevant comments; facial expressions; awkward silences; or changes in posture. These signal that your boss has more to tell you but is reluctant to do so.

2. By being more attentive to your boss's feelings than to your own, you will sense if he or she is frustrated or annoyed. If you have a gnawing feeling that something unstated lingers in the room, press for more information by saying, "Is something about this bothering you?" Or, "I want to do this job perfectly, do you have any suggestions?" This will tell your boss that what's important to him is equally important to you.

3. Before beginning any significant assignment ask your boss, "Here's how I see this project. Do you agree?" You don't want to finish an assignment only to hear "This isn't what I wanted!"

4. Senior managers loathe surprises. You might be unaware that a seemingly mundane matter could provoke a dispute between your boss and his or her peers. A brief note, phone call, e-mail, or drop-by visit to let your boss know "I'm sending this complaint to Marketing; is that OK?" can avoid embarrassing him.

5. Many bosses are uncomfortable giving negative performance reviews. They are tempted to gloss over deficiencies they fear will offend employees and create conflict. This is especially common when white men review minorities and women. Early in the discussion state how important it is for you to know exactly where you must improve. Say, "The more candid you are the more I'll benefit." This will reassure your boss that you will not report his directness as bias. Ask for specific examples. Do not become defensive; doing so could cause your boss to withhold the very advice that can advance your career.

6. Although they may seem self-assured, many bosses have insecurities similar to yours. They worry about their jobs, the advancement of peers, how they are being evaluated; and they are ambitious but realize the

pyramid is narrowing. These uncertainties make them acutely sensitive to behavior that reveals to them your loyalty, judgment, trustworthiness, and potential. "Can I count on you, will you embarrass me?" is an unstated but always present concern to a boss. Your daily actions must demonstrate that you hear and respect what is important to them.

7. What is important to your boss can seem so trivial, so outside the realm of business, that you might disregard it. Some bosses start 8 A.M. meetings at 7:55 A.M. Be there at 7:55 A.M.

Suzanne should not bring muffins.

8. Here is a particular insight for women. Fearful of being thought "unbusinesslike" if they engage in small talk, women often launch directly into the business at hand. Your boss might find this abrupt, even jarring. Take cues from men in the room. They often ease into business with banter about the weekend, industry gossip, or a news or sporting event. This small talk lasts a matter of seconds but lends a collegial touch to the meeting.

Suzanne (and you) might consider taking those same few seconds to ease into business. It's a personal touch many bosses appreciate.

NEVER FORGET WHY YOU WERE HIRED

Your Boss Recruited You for a Reason

Overlooks What's Important · Can't Manage Former Peers · Old Boys' Club Mentality

What You See

Katherine R., M.D., President, community hospital

I was recruited from one of the most respected northeastern medical centers to run this community hospital, which faces a budget crisis and the risk of losing its medical school affiliation. Two years ago the medical center had appointed me chief medical officer with the promise I would be named president when the CEO retired. I left there only because my boss decided he was not ready to retire the same week I was invited to interview for this job. He told me I was ready for the challenge of rescuing a hospital in trouble, and I decided to accept.

Female colleagues at the medical center were ecstatic for me, but some said they heard this place had a reputation for hiring and firing women doctors. The community hospital's former chief of radiology, a woman with a national reputation, called to tell me I should think carefully before accepting the position. When I pressed for specifics, she said her severance agreement prevented her from going further, but her warning was clear. I immediately asked for separate meetings with the board, medical and administrative department heads, and key attending physicians before I made a final decision.

I was reassured at every level that I was being recruited precisely because the hospital's future was at stake and I was the person to reorganize the place from the ground up. Board members, physicians, administrators, and community leaders pledged their support and were delighted when I agreed to come.

My first encounters with male colleagues were so positive that I began to wonder if the warnings I received were outdated or overly feminist. Indeed, these men assured me they wanted women physicians, including the former radiology chief, to succeed. They said they had pleaded with the female physicians to reconsider unpopular decisions. They told me their guidance was ignored, and the women plunged ahead aggressively, alienating colleagues, nurses, and administrators. The men seemed so disappointed that female physicians had left and so sincere in their support of my hiring that I became convinced they welcomed women in senior positions.

Several of the most respected male physicians quickly became my mentors, steering me through the challenges of running a community hospital. They named attending physicians and department chiefs whose support I should enlist before announcing major decisions.

Their advice made sense; I had seen administrators fail when they made abrupt changes, ignoring the privileges and opinions of key staff. My determination to reorganize every aspect of the hospital remains stronger than ever, but I'll do so by winning the support of those who built this place.

What Your Boss Sees

Lucas D., Board Chairman

Katherine seemed the answer to our problems. After our first meeting with her, we stopped interviewing. She came from a prestigious teaching hospital, had a fine reputation as a derma-tologist, had risen to manage physicians with huge egos, and, incredibly, had found the time to attend the two-month Harvard Advanced Management Program!

Within days of her arrival, she began making long overdue changes, and the board was certain our budget and affiliation problems were history. But, inexplicably, she gradually became tentative and reluctant to demand modernization from some of the older department chiefs. Our pathology department, for example, is a disgrace and has caused us legal and accreditation nightmares. I was convinced she would overhaul it immediately. But Katherine seems in awe of its chief and has left him alone. Her early improvements are becoming memories. If she doesn't begin doing what we need and want from her, we'll be forced to admit we made a mistake. How could someone so perfect for a job forget why we hired her?

MY DIAGNOSIS

Male mentors, deliberately or unconsciously, often advise women to proceed cautiously to avoid conflict: "You'll meet resistance here if you move too aggressively. Don't try to change things overnight." To avoid contro-versy, women are tempted to accept this advice and defer actions they were about to take.

When residential buildings in New York and other cities began converting from rental to cooperative ownership, male accountants typically advised women clients to remain renters and not purchase their apartments at insider prices. "Ownership is risky. What if prices fall? Also, your rent is lower than the maintenance charge you'll pay as an owner. Put your money into certificates of deposit; they're safer."

Women who listened and remained renters—and most I have spoken to did—were devastated when purchasers saw their apartments soar in value. "Even in this down market the apartment I was offered for $30,000 is worth $250,000, and I couldn't buy it if I wanted to" is a frequently heard lament.

Male mentors at work also generally advise women to avoid risk: "You don't want men to see you as overly aggressive. Be patient and move slowly; you'll win their support." Katherine—delighting the board with her early leadership—began denying the instincts that told her to move swiftly to control budgets, upgrade technology, and dismantle departmental fiefdoms. Instead, she listened to cautionary advice and forgot why the board hired her.

Most men I meet are genuinely devoted to the women they mentor and appear to revel in their successes. The few who deliberately undermine women with flawed advice are quickly detected and shunned. But my experience—in organizations and cultures across the world—is that the same mentor who encourages men to be bold is overly protective of women, restraining their instinct to act decisively.

ACTIONS I RECOMMEND

1. Never forget why you were hired. This is true for women and men. Katherine (and you) were hired because your strengths matched the organization's needs. You wouldn't have been hired if the enterprise was flourishing. You were brought in to make things happen. Don't let the variety of opinions you're going to receive divert you. Your boss's expectations must fill your head, not the restraining suggestions of others.

2. As a newcomer you must solicit and be receptive to constructive advice. To dismiss heartfelt guidance will mark you as arrogant and unworthy of support. But never forget that your ability to judge situations—your intuition—helped you win this job. Employ that gift to assess the advice you receive. Then let your instincts tell you which suggestions are in your best interest and which are inadvertently minimizing you.

3. Bosses like metrics. They expect measurable goals and specific steps employees plan to take to attain those goals, and they want them quickly. Bosses want employees to say to them: "This is where we are. This is where we're going. These are the obstacles to overcome. Here's when and how they will be surmounted. These are the benchmarks by which results will be judged."

4. Periodically report progress to your boss. "Here's what we've achieved to date and the actions we plan to take and deadlines we've set. Do you have any suggestions or concerns?" Don't wait for your boss to call you.

5. In both healthy parenting and healthy mentoring, there comes a time to say good-bye. This is difficult for parents and children as well as for mentors and those being mentored. Nurturing counsel has been shared and absorbed. Katherine (and you) must now put that wisdom to work. You alone—and not those offering suggestions—are being held accountable for the results expected of you. Your boss has no interest in the advice you've been given; he or she cares only about your results.

6. Katherine (and you) will be evaluated by an entire universe of associates. Each will have expectations of you, many of them divergent, some even conflicting. But the opinion of your boss transcends all others. If Katherine doesn't act on the chief of pathology and other problems she was recruited to solve, the board will act on her. Satisfy everyone except your boss and you will lose your job.

MANAGING IN A FOREIGN CULTURE

*Mexico May Be Minutes from San Diego,
but It's Not the United States*

| Rigidly Analytical | Arrogant and Dismissive | Selfish | Old Boys' Club Mentality | Refuses to Yield |

What You See

Edward F., Vice President, Quality Assurance, electronics manufacturer

My predecessor tried so hard to be seen as the "Friendly Gringo and Round Eye" that he let quality decline in our Mexican and Chinese plants. Our U.S. factories were forced to rework much of their production before it was shipped to customers. When he retired, I was promoted and told to make certain quality never slipped below 98.5 percent and to aim for zero defects by year-end.

Our Mexican and Chinese plant managers expected me to be just like the former head of Quality Assurance. They invited me to dinners at their favorite restaurants and planned to take me to some of the nearby tourist attractions. They seemed startled when I said I'd prefer to return to the plant after a quick bite and leave the sightseeing for another time.

During my initial visits, I quickly found their engineering didn't meet my standards and quality inspectors were passing products they should have rejected. When I began instituting stricter requirements, they acted as if I'd insulted their country. I don't care if we're in Milwaukee, Juarez, or Nanjing, my job is to ship products of the highest quality. I try to be respectful but leave relationships to the State Department. I'm here to stop rejects and am sorry if they see me as culturally insensitive.

What Your Boss Sees

Don H., Senior Vice President, Manufacturing

Ed is the most professional Quality Assurance manager I've ever met. He's been with us for ten years, and I handpicked him to run our Q.A. department. He's an officer in the American Society for Quality and is so respected that Underwriters Laboratories virtually always agrees when he requests approval for one of our new products.

He's so admired in the States that I ignored early reports from our Mexican and Chinese plant managers that his visits were creating problems. I ascribed their comments to the stricter standards he's enforcing. Once they saw quality improve, I figured they'd have as much respect for Ed as I do.

But we've gotten so many complaints that I sent our Human Resources vice president to Mexico and China to assess what's going on. He negotiates with our unions and is hardly a bleeding heart, but even he was troubled by Ed's behavior. Apparently Ed told graduates of Monterey's technical university—Mexico's

MIT—that freshmen at North Carolina State, his school, were better engineers than they were.

Chinese manufacturing supervisors and quality inspectors remained silent until our H.R. man convinced them that their comments would only strengthen the plant. Complaints began pouring out. Ed always criticized, never praising even though quality had begun to improve before he arrived and is gradually approaching that of our best U.S. plants. He also spoke down to them, was always too hurried to listen to their suggestions, continually questioned their data and never apologized when the data proved accurate, and laughed at some of their customs.

When Ed returned from China, I told him I was disturbed by what I'd heard, that his behavior was creating problems in two countries vital to our success. It was as though his passport and work visas had given him authority to mistreat people. I told him his behavior had to change, and quickly.

He became angrily defensive. "They don't have the same quality standards we do. The Mexicans are so tied to their families that they rush home during Christmas shutdown and never return. All their training is wasted, and their replacements make bad parts. The Chinese are farm workers who don't comprehend that electronic parts are fragile. I don't mistreat them; I just expect a quality product. That's why you sent me there!"

Our H.R. vice president and I have to find a way to retain Ed's commitment to quality without alienating two entire workforces. We'll outline specific ways he can raise standards while still treating people with dignity and respect. We'll learn pretty quickly if he can do that or is too rigid. I hope he can change and that employees in Mexico and China will see his value and accept him. But as good as Ed is, he's not as important as the goodwill we must have if our offshore plants are to be successful.

MY DIAGNOSIS

I frequently work at the overseas offices and factories of U.S. companies and am struck by how warmly some corporate representatives are greeted while others receive an icy, formal reception. Within moments of observing the visitors' behavior I understand why there is a difference.

Some come with the attitudinal equivalent of a smirk. Their behavior and tone are condescending. I often overhear comments like "I don't know what language people in this call center think they're speaking, but it isn't English." "This press worked just fine in our Milwaukee plant, and now it's useless." "Let me show you how we do it in the States."

Most corporations provide an orientation for employees going abroad. Executives in these organizations have heard horror stories about insensitive behavior and are determined to prevent it. But, once away from the United States, some corporate visitors become as arrogant as occupying soldiers.

There's a seductiveness in being the expert flown thousands of miles to impart knowledge. Restaurant owners in those countries wince when telling stories of boastful visitors holding court, surrounded by local employees.

Ed fails to realize that while the trip from the San Diego airport to a Tijuana factory takes less than an hour, he has crossed an international border and entered a new culture. Nor does he appreciate that most Mexican plants no longer house acres of young women hunched over primitive tasks. Teenage assemblers with swift hands have been replaced by skilled workers who operate automated equipment as sophisticated as any across the border.

The corporate visitor must now come as a partner to these more advanced facilities rather than as "the expert." His or her hosts expect that the change in role is accompanied by a change in attitude. A veteran Chinese manager told me, "In the beginning we were in awe of corporate staff; we were their apprentices. Now we can teach them if they will listen." Ed (and you) must carry expertise across borders with humility or endure a frigid welcome and find your ideas politely ignored.

ACTIONS I RECOMMEND

1. Until recently, cheap labor—not untapped sources of knowledge—drove jobs abroad. That's changed. Technology now blankets the world and is no longer reserved for the elite. Those who once fled to the United States to find opportunity no longer have to leave countries where General Electric, IBM, and other companies have built research facilities as elegant as any in Palo Alto. Two people in a Bangalore garage have the technology to invent the future.

2. Confidence is soaring across most borders. You will be welcome only if you arrive as both teacher and student. People will listen to you as avidly as you listen to them. They will pester your boss to send you frequently if they feel you regard them as valued colleagues. But they will quickly close the door if they sense even a hint of condescension.

3. Corporate visitors understandably are most comfortable with local managers who speak fluent English. But too often, visitors become dependent upon them, mistaking language fluency for superior job skills. You will quickly lose the respect of high performers if you don't look beyond language to determine if a manager is outstanding or mediocre. Take your time; you are likely to discover that many of the managers who can be of greatest help to you have dedicated themselves to their craft, hoping gradually to hone their English.

4. Employers in developing nations play an almost familial role in the lives of their people. At every level employees speak of the company as "part of us." Their feelings are reminiscent of pre-outplacement America. When my father told stories about the slaughterhouse in which he worked, he need only say "the place" and our family heard how much it defined him as a man.

    The enterprise still has that emotional significance in the offshore facilities I visit. Because the company is so entwined in their lives, employees seek to know the human being beneath your managerial persona. They are more interested in you than in your title. They want to know something of your history, of your family. They don't want you to judge them but to add your talents to theirs to build the enterprise that has made you part of their lives. Make certain your behavior on and off the job accurately defines you.

5. Once they sense your respect, offshore employees will look to you for guidance beyond the job. They will want you to suggest readings, classes they might take, and additional responsibilities to which they can aspire. You can also tactfully help them perfect their English.

6. Have the confidence to communicate basic thoughts in their language, asking them to correct you. Know something about their nation's history, culture, and current events. Experiment when dining. Don't be afraid to say, "That looks good, but I'm getting on a plane tomorrow. Should I try it or wait until next time?" You'll get a laugh—and appreciation. You are becoming one of the family, and your return to them will be eagerly sought.

7. Above all, remember you are visiting their country. You are not there as their superior, but as someone eager to share your knowledge and gain their insights. You will know you have succeeded when one of them invites you to his or her home. When I knocked at the door of a supervisor in Guangzhou, his prekindergarten daughter smiled at me and in English said, "Welcome, Mr. American man."

During the meal the girl would ponder and then point and say "cloud" or "food" in English. I was charmed but, later that night, realized no American child I know could say in Chinese, "Welcome, Mr. Chinese man." My respect for the supervisor and his family grew, as did my concern for what the global marketplace will demand of my children and grandchildren.

After a long day at her plant, a Chinese engineer told me, "Knowing each other as we do now, there could never be another war." I was touched and pray she's right. We can make our small mark on history if we go abroad determined to be welcomed visitors in a world that seems so alien at first, but, in time, proves to be remarkably like our own.

AVOID OVERSTATING PROBLEMS

Maybe the Sky Isn't Falling

What You See

Phillip T., Assistant Executive Director, children's welfare center

After twenty years as an attorney, mostly as a litigator, I was becoming burned out representing rich executives eager to become richer. So when I heard an announcement on public broadcasting about a nonprofit organization seeking someone with legal and managerial experience I called.

I was enthralled when I met the executive director and her staff, all of them committed to helping children and young adults lead productive lives. They took me through their day-care, preschool, and after-school programs; counseling center; and vocational training and job placement facilities. The place was alive with children, adolescents, young adults, teenage mothers, and volunteers of every age, race, and background. The more interviews I had, the more I realized I could finally be doing work

*of social value. It meant taking a huge pay cut, but I was over-
joyed when they offered me the job.*

*Dealing with combative legal clients who demanded instant
solutions had trained me to drill immediately to the heart of
a problem. To avoid misunderstandings, I stated all possible
choices and the pros and cons of each so that clients could
make informed decisions. I made certain they knew the risks
entailed in any decision they made.*

*I'm now in a very different world, but my training still
demands that I alert the staff whenever we run the risk of violating regulations governing agencies like ours. Working with
kids requires that you comply with a maze of state and federal
codes. Lawyers and the media leap at the chance to defend
children they allege are victimized by "unfeeling" agencies.*

*My job is to keep us out of trouble by complying with
those regulations. It upsets me that staff members I respect
are complaining that I invent fears that aren't real. They say
the same rules existed before I came and they had no viola-
tions. Just today one of the counselors said I'm turning us into
a bureaucracy. They don't realize that regulations aren't the
same. They're stricter, and organizations dealing with children
are under increased scrutiny. Look at community outrage when
a school, hospital, or social welfare agency fails to report sus-
pected child abuse!*

What Your Boss Sees

Shantal M., Executive Director

We were lucky to get Phil. Most of the other applicants were
single practitioners or were retired and had little energy.

Phil was in mid-career as managing partner of litigation at one of the city's most prestigious law firms. Many of our board members know him and were surprised he would leave his firm to come here. He said he wanted to repay society for all it had given him. I believed him then, and I believe him now.

I saw immediately that Phil could be a wonderful advocate for us. He anticipates problems before they arise. His ability to state differences without offending either side has helped us defuse problems with agencies that regulate us. Many of the officials at those agencies know him. With a phone call he handles problems that kept me busy for hours. His combination of legal and managerial experience has been invaluable to us.

But, he has a major flaw that is hurting him, and us. He tends to overstate the seriousness of problems. Every concern is urgent; every challenge is potentially disastrous; every complaint threatens our accreditation. The sky is always about to fall. He just told two of our counselors that they should speak with him before giving advice that could have legal implications.

People resent his interference and the tone of his warnings, and they are beginning to tune him out. I want Phil to identify potential problems and make certain we're complying with regulations. But he's got to stop crying "Fire!"

MY DIAGNOSIS

Some professionals—lawyers, auditors, compliance managers, and security officials—who think they stand alone between their organizations and impending danger believe they must pound their messages home. "You don't realize how serious this is. We could be in trouble if we don't act immediately."

This impulse to overemphasize risks is especially true when the professional is alone in an organization. If others with similar training were present to validate concerns, these concerns could be expressed less dramatically. The only lawyer on staff, Phil wants his fears taken seriously and so he states them gravely. But crying "Fire!" too often is eroding his credibility. Phil—and you—must bring risk into focus without being viewed as alarmist. There are ways to have your concerns heard and taken seriously.

ACTIONS I RECOMMEND

1. Overstatements quickly lose their audience. You will be excused, even considered watchful, if once, perhaps twice, you exclaim, "This could be a problem," only to see the risk fade. But your next warning could be met with skepticism.

2. If I believe a client might be putting itself at risk, I stimulate discussion rather than incite fear. "The staff reductions you're proposing fall heavily on long-service women. Can't you get the same savings by reducing head count at the new Spokane office?" That works much better than saying, "You'll be hit with age- and sex-discrimination suits that will keep you in court for years!" One invites discussion while the other creates defensiveness and reluctance to express an opinion that could prove wrong.

3. You were hired for your competence, experience, and credentials. Associates respect those attainments and

will pay attention to your advice. But you are also part of a team whose members will cease listening if your judgments are consistently negative and overheated.

4. If colleagues are beginning to disregard your warnings, ask yourself: "Am I controlling?" "Are people right when they call me bureaucratic?" "Am I becoming risk-averse and pessimistic?" "Am I an alarmist?" If the answer to any of these could be yes, let someone else open meetings with his or her concerns. You can agree, even add more detail, but don't always be the first to speak. If no one volunteers and you believe something must be said, do so with restraint. Understate, letting the facts speak for themselves without flourishes from you.

5. Observe how respected associates state their concerns: "Some of our boys are teasing Islamic girls about their head scarves. They're just being boys, but I've seen girls in tears, and it's got to stop. Let's develop a program that shows how painful it is to be teased. What do you think?"

The respected associate would certainly escalate his or her concern if there was little response, but would do so gradually, and only as high as necessary. "I don't want our Islamic kids to feel they're outsiders. We've got to come up with something, and soon." He or she didn't overstate to make a point: "We'll have Muslim protesters outside calling us infidels!" The associate wanted action, yet enlisted the views of others and didn't begin or end by crying "Fire!" Neither should Phil (or you).

6. Never wave credentials at associates. "I'm a lawyer (or CPA or former FBI agent), and *I* know . . ." will quickly turn allies into skeptics. A degree does not make someone infallible. Instead, express your fears in terms associates can understand and debate. Colleagues are eager to hear your professional opinion but will not allow your degrees to intimidate them.

7. Phil (and you) must anticipate looming problems; that's what managers do. But the tone of voice in which you alert associates to those problems will define you either as perceptive or an alarmist. Your bearing must convey a problem exists, but you can work together to solve it. Such demeanor will quickly earn you a reputation as one who combines watchfulness with a reassuring presence, not as someone on whom the sky is always falling.

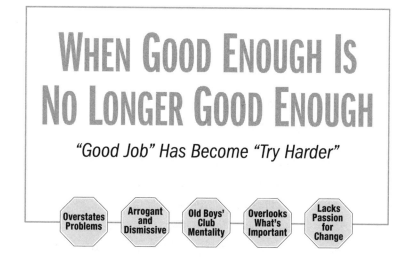

WHEN GOOD ENOUGH IS NO LONGER GOOD ENOUGH

"Good Job" Has Become "Try Harder"

Overstates Problems — Arrogant and Dismissive — Old Boys' Club Mentality — Overlooks What's Important — Lacks Passion for Change

What You See

Norman J., Underwriting Supervisor, insurance company

I came to this company fresh out of high school and learned underwriting from masters of the craft. Every young person here brings their questions to me. They know I'll help them find the answers they need.

My new boss arrived with an M.B.A. and three years' experience with a competitor. He lives and breathes systems and ratios but doesn't have a clue about the people we insure. He accuses me of being too lenient with clients we've had on our books for years. I know they're good risks, and so do the agents who bring them to us. But my boss insists we impose sharply higher premiums. To him they're not loyal clients, they're numbers on one of his charts. Doesn't he realize many of our insureds will go elsewhere when their rates increase?

What Your Boss Sees

Craig W., Vice President, Underwriting

hareholders are demanding that we be more profitable; that's why this company recruited me. I came from an organization that expected clients to pay premiums, which made business sense. It systematically evaluated every client, new and existing. Some clients emerged with lower premiums because they ran safe, ethical enterprises. Others were compelled to pay higher premiums because they were putting themselves, and us, at risk. Some protested, but remained because they eventually agreed we were being reasonable. Others left, some switching to this company for its lower premiums. I've given Norman software that proves his underwriting is loose and out of date. He just ignores it.

He is an old-fashioned underwriter who has known our older agents for years and been to their kids' weddings. They come to him with some very marginal clients because they know he'll underwrite them. His good old boy way of doing business worked when shareholders were less involved. Now financial analysts are hounding us for better results. We've got to increase premium income to satisfy them and our shareholders.

Norman's way was once good enough; now it's not. I'm going to recommend we offer him a severance package.

MY DIAGNOSIS

The bottom line has become a club wielded by financial analysts and shareholders. Companies are reminded relentlessly by those who've never stepped onto a sales or factory floor that their prices are too high, their products outmoded, their quality deficient, or their earnings per share too low. To regain shareholder favor companies are demanding higher productivity from every employee. Pressure on managers is relentless; in their dreams they hear "You're not adding value!"

Fickle consumers, price-shaving competitors, new businesses springing from the Internet, jobs flooding to China, and young managers fueled by an almost religious devotion to technology all demand that every employee produce more. Nothing is more painful in my work than hearing that a once competent manager is no longer good enough to meet these new demands.

Norman is at risk of becoming one of those casualties. As an employee, it is essential that you reinvent yourself frequently so that you are seen as part of your organization's future, not its past.

ACTIONS I RECOMMEND

1. Being called predictable would end my consulting career. Like Norman, I would be judged no longer good enough. The younger managers I mentor would yawn at my advice. I must continually reinvent myself if I am to remain sought after. To reinvent myself and remain relevant, I periodically step out of myself and imagine that "Bob has gone. What did he do that achieved little or nothing? What didn't he do that he should have done?" Looking at myself as a stranger, I quickly realize the power of habit. How reflexive it is to give the same advice, repeat the same anecdotes!

2. I struggle to resist old habits and discover more creative ways to mentor that are consistent with my character. I have no interest in questioning my deepest convictions. I simply want to be ready to make the changes the world and my clients demand of me.

Reinventing oneself is difficult. Momentum—plunging ahead as usual—is tough to arrest. It's reasonable to wonder "Why should I do things differently? I'm fine just the way I am."

You might remain the same, but the world won't. Work, and the way it's done, is changing feverishly. Students buy and sell website domains from dorm rooms. A woman in Bangalore answers your credit card questions. Cars that soon will be running on the interstate are being manufactured in Korean towns you've never heard of. Computer nerds carve tools and dies that once were the province of gruff European machinists.

If you don't reinvent yourself periodically someone across the world—or down the street—will take your job.

3. Don't be quick to say no to ideas that challenge your sense of order. Absorb what you're hearing. Listen for reasons to think "This idea might work." With a few modifications it might be the solution you are seeking. It is easy to become complacent at work and to see new ideas as complicating your routine. Let yes be your default word when presented with new ideas.

4. Fight the temptation to reply, "We've always done it this way." Or, "We tried that years ago and it flopped."

The world has changed so much that the once wild idea might have found its time.

5. Even if you work for a global company, think like an entrepreneur. Anticipate developments occurring just out of sight that will soon force their way into your department. Ponder how you're going to respond to them.

6. Walk as a first-time visitor through the space you manage and ask, "Why do we do things this way?" "Are we doing unnecessary work?" "With all our technology, why are we generating so much paper?" "Would anyone notice if we stopped distributing all those reports?" "Why do we do so much manually?" "Is there better use for this space?" Look closely at your employees and ask yourself if you are inspiring or deflating them.

7. Also ask, "What is the first thing visitors see and feel when they come here?" Before responding that the place looks fine, remember the countless times you walked past the spot on your kitchen wall before a potential buyer asked, "What's that stain?"

As recently as a year ago, Norman was good enough, but he isn't today. Don't risk joining him and others considered expendable as revenues shrink. Senior managers talk in astonishment of the number of top-flight people looking for work, some who use the new media to bring themselves to the attention of your boss.

Reinvent yourself and then look beyond your routine tasks, wondering how you are going to respond to what's out there, just over the horizon. Make certain you are not only good enough, you've become better.

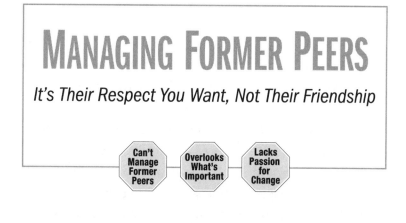

MANAGING FORMER PEERS

It's Their Respect You Want, Not Their Friendship

Can't Manage Former Peers — Overlooks What's Important — Lacks Passion for Change

---

What You See

Leslie H., Senior Vice President, Claims, insurance company

I was overjoyed when my boss retired and I was named head of Claims. Unlike Human Resources or Communications, Claims is a key operating unit in an insurance company, and our department had never been run by a woman. When I was called to the CEO's office, I half-expected to hear a man had been recruited to take over. When Dennis shook my hand and told me I was the first and only candidate, I vowed to make this the best department in the company.

Things haven't been easy. Male colleagues magnify every mistake I make, though none have been major and all probably would have been ignored if made by a man. That didn't surprise me; the executive floor is still a men's club. What has hurt is that many of my former peers—most of them women I grew up with in Claims—seem to resent my promotion. The man I replaced had become wary of "rocking the boat." We always talked of the *changes we would make if one of us were in charge. I was certain they would rejoice that one of their own had made it.*

As soon as my promotion was announced, I excitedly assembled my team to begin implementing changes we had been discussing for years. I saw this as a chance for women to prove they were as innovative and results-driven as men. But instead of bubbling with ideas, they seemed distracted and uninterested. The changes we vowed to implement aren't happening. Despite my pushing, things are moving slowly and the department seems flat. Neither Dennis nor Jamal, our chief operating officer, has said anything directly to me, but I sense impatience and disappointment in their passing comments.

What Your Boss Sees

Jamal R., COO

Dennis and I knew immediately that Leslie was the one to head Claims. In fact she really ran things as her boss neared retirement. She knows the business, is open to suggestions, has great rapport with the field, and is someone we've been developing because we need women in senior operating positions. Leslie was a perfect fit.

Days after Leslie took over, she told me they planned to roll out long-overdue programs and schedule trips to the field to win agency support. I thought the department had found the perfect manager to take it to a new level. But despite those early promises, she hasn't put her stamp on the department, and I'm not seeing results.

Men on this floor—including the very few who pushed for Leslie's promotion—have been asking if Claims has changed at *all. I've defended her, knowing that many of them disapproved of a woman running a department that had a direct effect on the bottom line. But I'm finding it hard to give examples of initiatives she's run with.*

I'm convinced her biggest problem is not separating herself from former peers. She's not a presence on the executive floor. She's never had an informal lunch with Dennis, me, or other officers up here. She never just drops in to discuss concerns or actions she's considering. Instead she continues to eat with her old crowd and socializes with them outside of work.

It took Leslie almost two months to move up here from her old office; she said she needed to be near her people. I was forced to order her to move, telling her she could meet with them frequently while still taking her place among senior management. She must build relationships with people on this floor if she's going to win the support she needs to succeed.

This morning Dennis told me he wants to discuss Claims, and I know that means he's losing patience with Leslie. Before that meeting I'll tell her she has a choice: she can retain the friendship of her employees or she can win their respect, but she cannot do both.

MY DIAGNOSIS

One of the most painful tests of leadership is managing former peers. The brief announcement of a promotion unleashes complex changes in working relationships. You are now boss of old friends. The friendly lunches, fantasy sports leagues, baby showers, gossip, and sharing of joys and sorrows, if not ended, are different. The first celebration or game you are not invited to will be a painful reminder you are now on the outside looking in.

Some of your closest former peers will resent you, wondering why you were chosen and they weren't. A few might take pleasure in your failing, even offering advice that isn't in your best interests. The most vivid illustration of peers holding peers in place is watching fishermen drop crabs into a bucket. The bucket needs no cover; escaping crabs are promptly snatched back by other crabs. One can almost imagine hearing a crab say, "If I'm stuck in this bucket, you're not going anywhere!"

Leaving any familiar position is not easy. Many cringe at the thought of being resented and losing the cozy feeling of being one of the gang. Managing any group can be a lonely experience, often making decisions only you see as necessary. Managing former peers—no longer being in the familiar web of friends—is doubly lonely.

If you want to leave the bucket and succeed in the higher position you've just won, be forewarned you must act quickly, and sometimes painfully.

ACTIONS I RECOMMEND

1. The moment your promotion is announced, meet with former peers who have suddenly become your subordinates. Tell them your affection and respect for them remain unchanged, but your involvement will be different. Ask for their understanding of the expectations senior management now has of you, letting them know some of those expectations will be personally difficult. You'll be spending more time with other executives, for

example, than with them. Tell them you will be unable to attend some of the social functions you enjoyed together through the years. Without your saying so, they must realize from the very outset that it is their respect you seek, not their friendship.

2. Fellow managers will evaluate how you move into their ranks: have you relocated your office, do you have lunch and informal conversations with them, are you a presence at meetings, and are you planning changes in your department, ranging from minor adjustments to a major reorganization? Your new colleagues do not expect you to act precipitously. But they will quickly determine if you are one of them or are more comfortable among your former peers. Your early actions must tell them you have chosen to lead.

3. Your right to lead will be judged by four audiences: the former peers you now manage, your new colleagues, top management, and, most important, you. While your basic character remains unchanged, the power you now have to affect the lives of others makes you a different person. Your self-assurance, your willingness to forego the comfort of being one of the gang, your confidence to conduct yourself as an equal of former bosses, and your determination to make things happen must convince everyone you have earned the right to lead.

4. Others will test that right. Former peers will seek favored treatment, new colleagues will poach on your territory, and senior managers will challenge your decisions in open meetings. Everyone will wonder if you are the right choice. Leslie (and you) must make it clear through actions that management made the perfect choice.

MANAGING DIVERSITY

It's No Longer a White Male Club

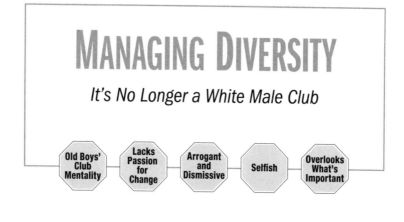

Old Boys' Club Mentality — Lacks Passion for Change — Arrogant and Dismissive — Selfish — Overlooks What's Important

What You See

James M., Controller, national supermarket chain

'm getting flack from my boss because Doug, an African-American manager working for me, isn't cutting it and I've suggested letting him go. My boss has occasional meetings with the guy and is impressed for reasons I don't understand. My boss also reminds me we're in a diversity push to recruit and advance minorities and can't afford to let one go.

I don't care if someone is blue, pink, or green; all I want is professional performance, and I'm not getting it. People in the Finance Department can see my disappointment with Doug. If I keep him they'll accuse me of reverse discrimination and will lose respect for him and for me.

What Your Boss Sees

Martin A., CFO

James is an outstanding controller and on track to replace me when I retire, but his response to my insistence that he work with Doug makes me wonder about his ability to lead a department that's got to be more diverse.

Our marketplace looks nothing like it did just months ago and will change even more in the years ahead. We're beginning to stock a wide variety of ethnic products and now do business with firms led by Hispanics, African-Americans, Asians, Muslims, East Indians, and Filipinos. The head of an Indian company recently looked around our conference table and whispered to me, "Where do you hide people of color?" He smiled, but I know he wasn't joking. That made me recommend to our CEO that we implement a diversity initiative. He agreed and told me to put teeth in it.

I interviewed Doug before we hired him and found him to be as qualified as any of the white candidates I met with. Quite frankly, I was surprised and delighted he was willing to join us. Our headquarters is miles from the nearest large city, and the community is almost entirely white. Doug and I periodically work together on Treasury issues, and I find his ideas and recommendations very sound. James had better understand we're in the process of change, and Doug is part of that change.

James has to demonstrate a breadth of awareness that goes beyond reading a balance sheet.

MY DIAGNOSIS

Through the years I've helped companies recruit and develop African-American managers. Many quickly became important contributors and advanced to key positions, but when considered for the very top jobs, most were passed over in favor of white men.

I recently interviewed about twenty black executives to ask why they believed so few of them were ascending to chief operating officer or chief executive officer. A key reason cited is that they don't feel included in the friendship circle that bonds their white associates. They don't participate in as many informal gatherings outside the workplace that foster personal connections.

The sense of shared intimacy—of being "one of us"—arises in the workplace but is nourished even more in personal contact on and off the job. For a variety of reasons—living in different areas, discomfort in some of the favored social settings, and unease at largely white events—African-Americans rarely develop the tight personal associations that cause a white senior officer to think "They'd be perfect for my team."

James might consider himself color-blind, but it remains unlikely he has the same personal comfort with Doug that he has with white male subordinates. The playfulness men engage in to lighten stress—sarcasm, boasting, or the trading of mock insults—becomes guarded when black men enter the room. Byplay then becomes cautious, not care-free, so artificial that it creates rather than relieves stress.

Like many white managers, James probably also finds it difficult to provide a blunt performance review to a black man, treading cautiously for fear of being seen as racially biased. As a result, Doug could leave such reviews unaware of shortcomings James would unhesitatingly convey to a white male subordinate. Actions he could be taking to correct those flaws remain stalled.

James is hardly alone in his inability to reach Doug as easily as he would a white man with whom he has more in common. Overt racism in organizations has declined dramatically, but unease between blacks and whites lingers. (A quick glimpse into a college or high school cafeteria reveals the racial separation that divides even the young.) This combination of personal distance and hesitation to confront creates an artificiality difficult to overcome. The ascension of African-Americans into the very top positions has been so slow that many I meet see themselves trailing emerging ethnic groups now entering the competition for leadership roles.

ACTIONS I RECOMMEND

1. James and his associates must make social events more welcoming to African-American employees, soliciting their thoughts before a site is selected. He must reassure Doug that his presence is eagerly sought and ask if the occasion and setting are agreeable to him. Clearly, everyone must have a voice in these choices, but Doug's cannot be overlooked.

2. James must begin by admitting to himself that he feels freer to criticize white male subordinates than he does Doug. He must say to himself, "My primary obligation as manager is to develop my people to their

fullest potential, and that includes Doug." This means conducting rigorous performance reviews, providing candid assessments of strengths and shortcomings, offering guidance, and inquiring about Doug's concerns and aspirations. He must take the risk that senior management can be trusted to judge when his forthrightness is in Doug's best interest and when it crosses the line into bias.

3. James would be a better manager of a diverse workforce if he understood that many African-Americans think they are judged differently than white associates. Most I interviewed, for example, feel they must be more tentative than white peers when disagreeing with a white senior manager. They also believe they are labeled implementers rather than strategic thinkers. They cite suggestions they offered that were overlooked, yet approved moments later when made by a white associate. They feel themselves to be outsiders, rarely becoming "one of us" when leaders are chosen.

4. Organizations will succeed in the global marketplace to the extent their workforces become microcosms of that universe. Customers of every race and ethnicity believe they are better understood when greeted by familiar faces. Doug brings with him a different life experience and vision that will enrich the company if he believes he—and other perennial outsiders—are welcome at the very top. James can strengthen his company by finding ways to be more welcoming to Doug, inviting him into that circle from which leaders emerge.

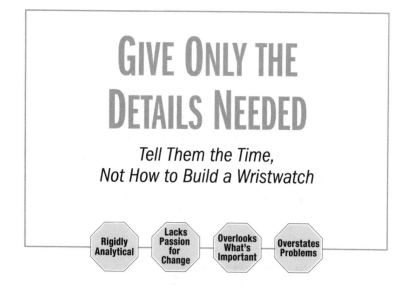

GIVE ONLY THE DETAILS NEEDED

Tell Them the Time, Not How to Build a Wristwatch

Rigidly Analytical · Lacks Passion for Change · Overlooks What's Important · Overstates Problems

What You See

Jordan C., Director of Administration, Financial Services Group

Like all investment firms, we've automated every function possible, trimming clerical staff to a fraction of the size it was just a few years ago. But the back office is still critical to our operations. Every transaction must be error free, and that still takes trade processors, branch control and work-flow staff, new accounts clerks, customer service specialists, and other administrative people who take responsibility once the client and broker have completed their trade.

I never expected the pay or praise our sales force and analysts receive. But they couldn't do their work without the efforts of back-office employees who are ignored by brokers who pass them in the hallway. My people complain to me about the lack *of respect they receive, but I never tell them that I feel just as slighted at the few senior management meetings I'm invited to. Analysts and brokers are listened to avidly as they discuss market forces and the products they're recommending, but I'm hurried through my report, often without a single question or word of thanks. I sometimes think senior management would be relieved if a computer could replace me at meetings.*

What Your Boss Sees

Todd B., Senior Partner

Jordan reports to me, and I do tell him how important he and his people are to the firm. But what sets us apart from competitors is our team of analysts—the best on Wall Street—and our tigers, the brokers out there winning and holding clients. Back-office work is not glamorous, and all I expect is that it smoothes the way for our primary function, making money for our clients and the firm.

So when Jordan gives an elaborate explanation of administrative functions he loses our interest. We need him to give us an overview—that his department is automating trades, importing best practices of other back offices, and providing data even more quickly to our people and to the agencies regulating us. We don't need to hear how many transactions a trade processor handles in an hour! He overwhelms us with data we haven't asked for. He's already lost the interest of some people and will be ignored by the rest if he doesn't give a concise report instead of numbing us with details.

MY DIAGNOSIS

Analytical people—convinced that success or failure lies in the details—are upset when data that thrill them bore listeners. Frustrated, they leave meetings worried, "If managers don't understand the data, how can they plan strategy! It drives me nuts when management requests an overview without too many statistics."

The most visionary strategic thinkers know that sooner or later they must comprehend the details. It's not data they're impatient with, it's how those numbers are presented. To present analytical information, you must have the timing of a stand-up comic to know when you're losing your audience. There are ways to provide statistics while holding their interest.

ACTIONS I RECOMMEND

1. Dole out details in small doses. Only the most analytical are able to sit patiently through a lengthy report dense with numbers. State your central theme and the most important facts underlying it. Then invite questions and comments before proceeding.

2. A presentation is a dialogue, not a monologue. Presenters lose their audience when they speak in pages instead of brief paragraphs. To hold the attention of a hard-pressed group, frequently ask, "Have I given you enough information? Do you need more?" Or, "Unless you want more data, I'll move on." Or, "Interrupt me if I'm giving too many details or not being clear." This encourages listeners to participate rather than squirm.

3. The younger the audience the greater its impatience. When speaking to young employees, be brief, almost staccato. "Sound bites" were unknown when President Kennedy could speak for nearly an hour about missile sites in Cuba. Today, his speechwriter would suggest a twenty-minute wrap-up or the audience would change the channel.

4. Avoid the temptation to add just one more fact. "I just couldn't stop myself. I could see they were getting restless but wanted to make certain they had enough information." Because I often feel that same temptation, as a personal reminder I occasionally write on my notes "KYMS"—"Keep your mouth shut!" And I do.

Jordan (and you) should scribble your own personal reminder. It is better to be intercepted after a meeting and asked for more data than to face a sea of glazed eyeballs. They want information in manageable doses. Tell them the time, not how to make a wristwatch.

PART 2

Emotions You Arouse in Others

Bosses don't dwell in a vacuum; they hear what associates say about you. They listen especially carefully if they are considering making you an even more important part of their management team or if, conversely, they have begun to question your value. Opinions of you from deep within the organization filter up to them and are taken seriously.

Chief executive officers seek to establish a culture—a belief system—that permeates and defines their organization. They see that culture as a personal legacy and will not entrust it to someone who would allow it to unravel. I'm still occasionally startled when a senior officer tells me why someone is being passed over for promotion or let go, thinking "That can't be the *real* reason." The missteps recounted seem to have little to do with work. It isn't until I hear the emotion in a boss's voice when they say, "He's just *not right* for us," that I realize the feelings the employee aroused have everything to do with work.

In justifying a decision to dismiss or deny promotion to an employee, a senior officer will cite business judgments and decisions that proved wrong. But if the employee had enjoyed his or her confidence, the boss would have worked with that employee to avoid or correct those mistakes. Something in the employee's behavior or attitude caused the boss to lose trust, and with it the willingness to offer a helping hand.

The following case studies will describe how to avoid stirring emotions in others that could make you "not right" for the job.

HUMOR THAT ISN'T FUNNY

If That's a Joke, Why Am I Bleeding?

Harmful Humor · Selfish · Refuses to Yield · Overlooks What's Important

---

What You See

Chuck M., Creative Director, advertising agency

This is a high-pressure job, and I find humor a great way to lighten tension. I've always had a good sense of humor, which is how I moved from writing jokes for a campus magazine to copywriting. Just recently the head of our agency said my comments were offending colleagues and I had to stop. When I told him I was trying to get people to chill out, to stop being so tense, he said I wasn't being funny, I was being hurtful and interfering with work. I think he's wrong and intend to get the opinion of my buddies when we have some free time.

What Your Boss Sees

Antonio C., Agency President

Chuck has a sarcastic edge, and what he thinks is funny sometimes draws blood. There is lots of pressure at our shop. We've just taken on two big clients and have to prove they made the right choice. Humor has its place; many copywriters are would-be stand-up comics and love to banter. Some of our most successful ads are lighthearted. But there's a difference between a funny aside and a barb.

As creative director, Chuck has writers and artists working for him, many of them young and somewhat insecure. I watch their faces and can see that his sarcastic comments hurt and sometimes stop the creative process. They are just getting the handle on an approach when Chuck says something he thinks is witty. It's not, and everything stops. If he doesn't cease trying to be a comedian, he'll be out of here.

MY DIAGNOSIS

Stress can tie the creative process into knots. Lighthearted humor can reduce frustration, channeling everyone's energy into the job rather than into anxiety. But humor can also have an angry edge, creating more resentment than relief. Men, especially, find sarcasm witty: "Oh, look who finally woke up and favored us with her annual contribution!"—while the recipient, especially a subordinate, can only wince.

Some managers find it easier to use humor as a disciplinary tool than to be direct. Annoyed with mistakes, their attempts at humor can have a cruel edge: "And Wharton awarded you an M.B.A. for that kind of thinking!" Although said with a smile, the remark is as painful as a slap.

Irritation disguised as humor generally results in an employee thinking "If he's trying to be funny, why am I bleeding?" There are times to use—and not to use—humor as a management tool.

ACTIONS I RECOMMEND

1. Sarcasm never wins. If your humorous quip could be heard as cutting, leave it unsaid. "Oh, good afternoon!" addressed to a slightly late subordinate is not funny, and it hurts. Deal directly—and privately—with the lateness. "Our meetings start at eight, so please be here on time" does the job without a sting.

2. Sense the tone of a meeting. Look at faces; listen to voices. Is the interaction stimulating or hostile? Your feel for what's happening will tell you when pressure is fostering innovation and when it's sucking oxygen from the room. If frustration is strangling progress, your lighthearted comment can offer relief and a new approach. But if you feel the clash of ideas is beginning to yield something exciting, don't interrupt. When the remark you're about to make could be received as "We're on the edge of a breakthrough and his stupid joke stops everything!"—don't make it.

3. Some managers, especially men, attempt humor when rising emotions make them uncomfortable, provoking them to blurt, "Maybe we should invite a shrink to these meetings!" The spirited exchange of ideas becomes embarrassed silence. Everyone gets your message: "Enough truth. Let's get back to being superficial."

4. Humor in the workplace is both an asset and a liability. It can be a pressure valve, allowing everyone to unclench. It can also be barbed and ill-timed. Listen to your intuition before attempting levity. If in doubt leave comedy to the professionals.

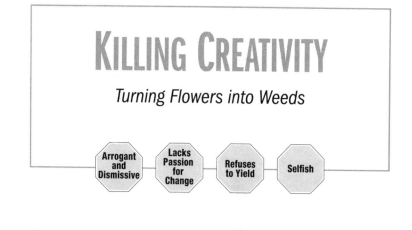

KILLING CREATIVITY

Turning Flowers into Weeds

Arrogant and Dismissive • Lacks Passion for Change • Refuses to Yield • Selfish

---

What You See

Laura S., Vice President, Textbook Marketing, publishing company

At age thirty-three, I'm the oldest member of my department. Many of my people have not been out of college long and are in their first jobs. I've had to remind them we're running a company, not a sorority or fraternity. They have to focus on their jobs and not on their social lives, act professionally, dress appropriately, be on time, and keep gossip to a minimum.

Our job is to set the stage for our sales force. We publish textbooks and face competition from every direction. Faculty members sell books we give them free. Students download material from our books and often get through the term without buying a copy. Competitors find hot young scholars and feed them book ideas. I'm sure my staff thinks I'm too demanding, but this century-old company is at risk and my job is to make certain we increase sales and regain market share. If I'm tough on them, it's for their own good.

What Your Boss Sees

Shannon D., Senior Vice President, Marketing

Turnover in Laura's department is the highest in our firm. That's partly because this is the first job for most of her people, and they aren't accustomed to life inside a professional setting. We deliberately run a fairly loose organization, but we do have rules and it's Laura's job to enforce them—but not with an iron hand. Other departments also hire people fresh out of school and manage to develop them. I started here in the mail room and worked my way up. Some of my early ideas embarrass me now, but my bosses kept encouraging my creativity. I doubt Laura does that.

Laura is still in her early thirties but thinks like someone much older. She's more a disciplinarian than a leader who nurtures new ideas. She rarely has anything positive to say about her people and never gives them exposure to senior management or takes them to sales meetings. She claims they would embarrass themselves and her, but I've had lunch with some of her people and find their ideas fresh and exciting. Sure, some suggestions are impractical, but many are exactly what our salespeople want. As young as she is, Laura might be too rigid to inspire creative people.

MY DIAGNOSIS

Laura has a very tough balancing act. She must make mature professionals out of people fresh from school without discouraging their creativity. This is easier said than done.

Young people complain about work requirements they consider mindless. "Every day at other firms is business casual. Why do we have to wear suits or dresses just because we might be summoned to a senior staff meeting? They want to see my work, not inspect my wardrobe." Or, "I got chewed out for being twenty minutes late even though I worked all day Saturday." Or, "They told me to leave my iPod home. I'm alone at a computer most of the time, what's the big deal!"

But their harshest complaints are reserved for managers whose intolerance for new ideas stifles creativity: "'That doesn't fit our business model' is my boss's typical response to almost every suggestion I make." Or, "If I hear 'that's impractical' one more time I'm out of here." Or, "If Bill Gates started here, he'd have been told, 'Be realistic; there's no market for this thing you call Windows!'"

Creative people excel under a manager who combines discipline with encouragement, helps them understand they are not squandering creativity by dressing appropriately and being on time, and teaches them how to present ideas to an audience wondering what this kid can tell them.

Fearful the bubbling spontaneity of her staff will embarrass her in front of other managers or sales executives, Laura responds by tightening her control and imposing stricter rules. Her staff becomes resentful and turns in work that's safe, not creative. Her department lags behind others in a company where the emphasis is on bold, exciting ideas. She may lose her job if she doesn't find ways to help her people become businesslike without stifling their creativity.

ACTIONS I RECOMMEND

1. Rules, written and unwritten, hold a society together, and a company—like a city—is a society. The successful manager of creative people must have the patience to apply those rules with a light touch, achieving both appropriate behavior and flair.

2. Here's one example I saw of stubborn behavior bending to a light touch. The young designer of wildly popular jewelry refused to wear safety glasses when soldering gold and silver samples, saying, "They're uncomfortable." Or, "These pieces are so small I can't see them through goggles; I'll be careful." (What she didn't add was "and I look terrible in glasses.") She ignored management requests to wear eye protection. Those requests became orders that escalated to demands and then threats, all without success.

At an impasse, management feared losing her but knew ignoring safety glasses would set a precedent others would follow. Impatient with her refusal to obey a sensible rule, several managers said, "Fire the brat!" Others knew if she left she'd be followed by jewelry retailers across the country.

The next day a senior designer came to work wearing an eye patch. "Oh, my God, what happened to your eye?" the young designer blurted. "I burned it while soldering earrings I'm designing," he replied. As she gazed in horror, he lifted the patch to reveal a perfectly healthy eye and said, "I don't want you to lose your eye." The following day—company rules and creativity intact—the young designer donned safety glasses.

You might agree with those who said fire the brat, but managing creative people is different than overseeing an assembly line. Meeting productivity targets without dimming the creative spark will test your patience. But one luminous idea can reshape a balance sheet. Look at the iPod.

3. Before rejecting an idea or tossing back a first draft, ask yourself if this is so great a departure that it scares you. What if it anticipates a product that will excite consumers? You want employees to find that point where marketable concepts and visionary ideas meet. Don't overcontrol; a heavy hand yields uninspired work. "She'll just tear apart what you turn in anyway, so why try?" Managing talent requires a gentler touch, shaping work into something both relevant and exciting.

4. Everyone wants to be taken seriously and to win approval. Creative people put themselves at risk by producing work that straddles the line between safe and bold, between acceptance and rejection. Their need for recognition is even greater. Creative work demands more of a manager than a quick skim. Talented people expect their managers to dig into their work so that criticism or praise reveals an understanding of what they are attempting. They recognize a cursory glance at their work and resent the comments that follow.

5. Eagerness for recognition can be satisfied in other ways. Expose employees to senior management. Sit back and let them introduce ideas. Don't worry that your boss will wonder why he or she needs you. Your boss knows

it's your leadership that attracts and holds people capable of captivating a meeting.

6. Any organization can appear monolithic, caring about nothing but the bottom line. So meet frequently with creative people. They must be reassured their voices are heard, that their work is shaping the company and its products. Cite specific innovations and sales achievements that resulted from their efforts.

7. Creative people can appear out of step with those in more traditional jobs. They require a manager who will defend them when more conservative associates criticize them. They also need a boss who is quick to tell them when their behavior is inappropriate. The ideal leader of creative people must strike a balance between championing their achievements and demanding that they observe the rules of the organization. Laura must find that balance or her replacement will.

WHEN LAID-BACK IS SEEN AS NOT CARING

You Think "Low Key"; Your Boss Thinks "Lazy"

Refuses to Yield | Can't Manage Former Peers | Overlooks What's Important | Doesn't Delegate

---

What You See

Brendan W., Help Desk Supervisor, state environmental agency

My boss is a former Marine and expects me to manage as he does, which is loud. I'm not like that. I manage by quietly telling people what needs to be done and expecting them to do it. On weekends I play in a garage band, and we're always on the same page just by a glance, gesture, or quiet comment. I'm that way at work, and my people get the job done and seem happy.

What Your Boss Sees

Paul V., Director, Information Technology

Brendan runs our Help Desk, which everyone calls when they have a computer problem. They want solutions and want them now. If callers don't get help from Brendan they call me, and I periodically hear complaints like "We've been down for an hour, and Brendan's people can't be found!" Or, "It would take someone thirty seconds to tell me why I keep getting an 'error' message. Why don't they get back to me?"

Brendan sees himself as laid-back, but I think he's uncomfortable leading a staff because he'd rather be liked than respected. Everyone calling him has a problem they regard as urgent, but I don't think he can spell the word. His previous boss told me to be patient, that Brendan gets the job done in his own way. I think I was being politely told I was no longer in the Marine Corps and to let Brendan run the Help Desk without too much supervision from me.

I have the entire IT Department to manage and would leave Brendan alone if I weren't getting complaints. The behavior he views as laid-back others see as indifference and not caring about the agency. A manager must respond with urgency when callers are clamoring for help. If Brendan wants to be laid-back, let him buy a surfboard and move to California.

MY DIAGNOSIS

Every organization I work with has its Brendans, most of them younger men and women who regard hard-nosed managers as relics out of touch with the new workforce. Most laid-back managers insist they hold their people accountable but do so in a more casual manner, declaring that "just because I don't shout or pound the table doesn't mean I'm not demanding." Indeed, many do use a lighter touch and get the job done as well as or better than older associates.

If you employ this lighter touch, you could be perceived by more traditional managers as not taking your job seriously. Brendan's boss, for example, sees being laid-back as an excuse for not holding people accountable. He can point to complaints he receives from Help Desk customers. It would be out of character for Brendan to become hard-nosed. But to eliminate complaints and convince his boss there is another way to manage, he must find a middle ground between casual and autocratic.

ACTIONS I RECOMMEND

1. If you sense coworkers are questioning your seriousness, ask a trusted associate if your informal manner is being perceived as laziness or reluctance to manage effectively. If told people have voiced doubts, you must take immediate steps to demonstrate that there is a solid managerial core beneath your affability.

2. Brendan should begin by quickly meeting with each of his in-house customers, asking for examples of Help Desk failures. He and his staff must take those complaints seriously, putting procedures in place to assure they don't reoccur. Subsequent calls to the Help Desk will be a test of Brendan's leadership. Callers will be wondering "Is he an effective, but low-key manager or one that doesn't care?" The Help Desk's responsiveness is the only answer that matters.

3. After making certain your team is focused on sharply improved performance, assure your boss you are as demanding as the most rigorous managers, but in your own way. Explain you get better results by treating people as responsible adults. Describe steps you take to hold people accountable. Coupled with very few complaints, this brief statement of your beliefs will provide the reassurance he or she will need if others question your management style.

4. Realizing that some members of your team might view your courtesy as a weakness to be taken advantage of, periodically reveal through your behavior that you can be as tough as any old-line manager. Brendan, for example, must demonstrate to those calling the Help Desk that their problems will be corrected promptly. If not, they are to immediately call him, and he will deal with those responsible. Any employee who mistakes respect for weakness will be disciplined.

5. Senior executives expect you to treat employees fairly. They want high morale as much or more than you do. But they also want their managers to get the job done quickly and within budget. Complaints about you quickly filter upward as complaints about them. Brendan's boss doesn't want it said of him that "he doesn't control his people very well, does he?"

6. Bosses will doubt a manager's competence if an alleged concern for people looks more like reluctance to discipline marginal performers. Managing well means balancing well: treating people with dignity and respect while holding them to high performance. Brendan (and you) can be laid-back but lead with a steel core.

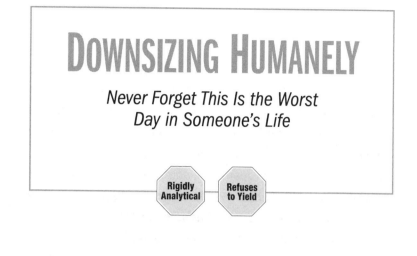

DOWNSIZING HUMANELY

*Never Forget This Is the Worst
Day in Someone's Life*

Rigidly Analytical **Refuses to Yield**

What You See

Kristine B., Regional Vice President, Branch Banking, multistate bank

I was promoted to attain two objectives: upgrade our branches and cut expenses by 7 percent this year and an additional 5 percent next year. Other goals and objectives are secondary. I've been given latitude and support by senior management but was cautioned they would expect results quickly.

In three weeks I visited virtually all the branches in my region and found most of them shared the same problems. Work flows, policies, systems, and the general conduct of business hadn't changed much from my days as an executive trainee in our downtown Evansville branch. It's as though time stood still while I was working my way up through our Trusts, Estates, and Premier Business Divisions.

Most managers are in their late fifties and early sixties, and some tellers are even older. Their resistance to the systems we're installing is clear from their questions. I conducted meetings at every branch after closing hours to tell staff about our initiatives and to hear their ideas and concerns. I'm their new boss, but that didn't stop many from complaining that meetings should be held during business hours, not on their time. I heard doubts about the new Oracle system but no fresh ideas.

While a few younger managers and tellers expressed enthusiasm for the innovations we've launched, most staff made their resentment clear: Things are going fine, customers aren't complaining, so why change? They don't appreciate that younger, busy customers will not tolerate long lines, teller positions deserted at lunch hour, ATMs that are frequently down, or managers unfamiliar with new banking instruments and technology.

They didn't seem to care that our branches aren't as busy, our customers are aging, and our market share has declined throughout the past decade. I believe I can make converts of many of our younger employees, but most long-service people just sat there looking bored when I described novel approaches our competitors are taking. If they think seniority will protect them from branch closings, they're wrong.

Senior management has given me a green light to modernize and cut costs, and that's what I'm going to do.

What Your Boss Sees

Jasmine R., Senior Vice President, Human Resources

Kristine is one of our best and brightest and has potential to rise to the very top. But her handling of the staff cuts she just submitted can make or break her. She intends to reduce staffing in her branches by more than 12 percent. That's a lot of people, most of them older and with long service.

I know many of those likely to be affected, and some have children who are lawyers or they know lawyers who have made this a litigious society. Cuts must be made and expenses reduced if we are to compete. But these are human beings with long service, and our bank is very much in the public eye. A few nasty court cases or messy human-interest stories, and our market share will shrink even further. My staff and I will be deeply involved in all these terminations, and I will stay very close to Kristine, counseling her throughout the process. But senior management will be judging her, not me, and she will rise or fall on the outcome of this downsizing.

MY DIAGNOSIS

Downsizing, outplacement, job abolishment, outsourcing— different words but all saying someone has been deemed unessential. The impact of job loss generally falls most heavily on older, long-service employees for many reasons. They typically earn more than younger associates at the same level, are often less dexterous and familiar with technology, and impose a heavier burden on workers' compensation, pensions, and medical coverage.

Every day I meet with employees described as older— many barely out of their forties—who are convinced they will be gone after the next round of terminations. Most are too young to retire and too old to find other employment easily. I also meet caring bosses who are the ones who must summon someone they've known for decades to tell them "I'm so terribly sorry, but . . ." Both to avoid allegations of age discrimination and for simple human decency, bosses must treat those losing their jobs just as your grandmother told you long ago: "as you would want to be treated."

When I was first promoted to manager, my wise and compassionate boss said, "You can now hire and fire. For a judge, capital punishment means killing someone. For you, capital punishment is firing someone. And remember, you don't usually fire a person, you fire a family."

I recount that wisdom to clients contemplating sweeping job cuts or when they've become impatient with a long-service employee seen as "a pain in the butt."

ACTIONS I RECOMMEND

1. Let's start with that one employee seen as an underperforming pain. Examine his or her past performance reviews. I've read hundreds, and even those of marginal employees are replete with "Consistently Meets Expectations" or its equivalent. Managers either ignored the deficiencies of these employees or were unwilling to discuss them in a candid performance review. Through no fault of your own, you've inherited a problem your predecessors let fester for years.

   Unlike them, you have no choice. You can meet budget only by eliminating underperformers, and this is your least productive employee. Keeping that person would be unfair to those getting the job done. But your conscience tells you prior managers are more to blame than the employee. Would that person now be a model employee if someone long ago had put them on warning and provided a performance improvement plan? It doesn't matter; they didn't.

2. Begin by canvassing other managers, asking if they have an opening your employee could fill. Level with them, recounting the employee's many flaws. It might be that one of them recalls strengths that can be utilized in another department.

3. If no one will touch them, at least you've tried. Then go to Human Resources to ask if the employee qualifies for early retirement. Explain that through the decades no one placed anything in the file but "Meets Expectations," and you believe fairness and possible legal action call for the least painful exit.

4. It might be that bending early retirement policies for this employee would establish a risky precedent. If so, press for a generous severance package.

5. Throughout this painful journey, never forget that after stripping away euphemisms like "you aren't being fired; your job is being abolished," you are *firing* someone, an act nearly as devastating as the loss of a family member. Explore every alternative, as you hope someone will for you someday.

6. If you're compelled to dismiss not one but many employees, follow the same steps. Canvass for openings in other departments, explore early retirement possibilities, assist in finding jobs elsewhere, and, finally, advocate generous severance packages. You are not being a bleeding heart. You are protecting your company from legal action, and, more important, proving you are a compassionate human being working for a caring employer.

7. Explain that Human Resources will provide assistance with résumés, job referrals, letters of recommendation, and practical advice on handling interviews. Make certain such programs are of high seriousness so that employees are satisfied they are being given practical help in going on with their lives.

8. When forced to make extensive job cuts, speak individually with everyone affected and then bring them together for a group meeting. These dreadfully painful encounters, fraught with the possibility of protests and threats, cannot be avoided. The meetings will be met either with derision or grudging acceptance, depending on how you and the others who are taking this action are assessed as human beings.

9. Your organization's attorneys undoubtedly will recommend against a group meeting, but I have found that employers who stand before all those affected are largely acknowledged as "at least having the decency to face us."

I have attended too many of these encounters and have yet to see caring managers treated with anything but respect, however grudgingly. Conversely, those who hide behind politically correct euphemisms, including "no one is being fired; we're just eliminating some jobs" are despised.

The faces of those leaving the building for the last time tell the story. You can read management's compassion, or lack of it, on those faces. Some are contorted in painful acceptance, others in fury. If those affected sense your empathy and pain, if they trust that the organization exhausted every possibility to avoid lay-offs and has provided generous career assistance and severance plans, they will emerge wounded, but without malice and hunger for revenge.

Kristine has a job to do, but throughout, she must conduct herself knowing that one day she too could be on an outplacement list.

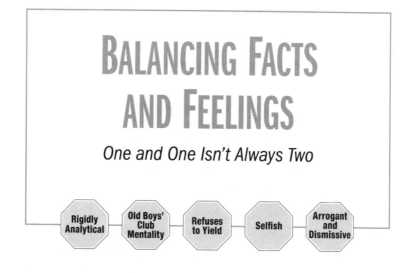

BALANCING FACTS AND FEELINGS

One and One Isn't Always Two

Rigidly Analytical — Old Boys' Club Mentality — Refuses to Yield — Selfish — Arrogant and Dismissive

What You See

Ernest K., Manager, Product Engineering, appliance manufacturer

I have little patience for people who lack precision and discipline, who talk about "sensing what the customer wants." I deal with facts, not feelings. Feelings don't build products. Yesterday I corrected a female industrial engineer who complained our new productivity rates were hurting employees' morale. Hurting morale! If their jobs were outsourced, they'd really have morale problems. I laughed and told her we were considering demanding even higher productivity, and she looked like she was going to cry. Doesn't she realize if we don't build our products faster and cheaper, someone else will? Can't people handle the truth? Things are either right or wrong; one plus one always equals two.

What Your Boss Sees

David C., Senior Vice President, Operations

Ernest is a great engineer, and it shows in the products he's developed. Before he came we were never leading-edge, but now we are. He wants a management role in manufacturing, and he's earned it. But there's a lot of ambiguity in a factory; the wrong mix of people on the floor can stop production. For Ernest there is no gray, everything is either black or white. He has no patience for anything but facts. Just this week one of our brightest young engineers threatened to quit after leaving his office. And it's not the first time he's humiliated a top performer. How can I put someone so coldly analytical in a job where a manager has to get hundreds of personalities to work together?

MY DIAGNOSIS

Engineers, accountants, actuaries, and others who thrive on data often are at a loss when managing a diverse population. Emerging from a world of numerical certainty, they fail to realize that one plus one does not always equal two, that pairing two marginal performers could yield zero.

If Ernest hopes to manage a wide array of employees, he must first win the loyalty of those reporting to him. They will quickly judge if he's more interested in facts than in them. While applauding his analytical prowess, they will cooperate halfheartedly unless he finds ways to reach them. Until he does, they will remain a fractured gathering and not a team.

The objective so clear to Ernest is being viewed by his employees through different prisms, some of them far less quantitative than his. Ernest's challenge is to find ways to merge his analytical strengths with intuitiveness— "gut feel." Only then can he win the trust and support of the range of personalities standing between him and his vision.

ACTIONS I RECOMMEND

1. Managing diverse personalities is more an art than a skill. The analytical manager, so comfortable with data, will quickly learn that employees can defy logic. Seemingly safe assumptions about people often prove wrong. Those you count on will disappoint, while those you expect little from will flourish. The complex project will unfurl easily, and the simple task will become a nightmare.

Resist relying solely on facts, and learn to observe changes in your employees' moods and comments. Ask yourself, "Why am I finding doubt and resistance when the numbers tell me I'm right?"

2. This in no way implies that you should ignore data or the analytical skills that got you hired. It does mean striking a balance between your intellect and the emotions of those around you. No one needs to tell you that you are judged by the numbers your organization produces. But be equally aware your employees have the power to send those numbers up or down.

3. To manage diverse personalities, develop intuitiveness to accompany your analytical skills. Intuitiveness, or gut feel, can be acquired by even the most data-obsessed savant. Obey that hunch—that insight lodged more in your stomach than in your head—that tells you the numbers might be correct but something about the report doesn't *feel* right.

   Intuition is that internal voice telling you to trust someone you barely know. It is being shown a house and knowing at once you want to live there. It is coming back from a first date confident you've met the person you want to marry. It is acting with little data, knowing you are right. It is rejecting advice because your gut feel distrusts it.

4. Successful managers absorb hard data and intuition and weave those facts and feelings into decisions. They never dismiss that internal voice because it isn't supported by data. They take it seriously enough to dig deeper into the data before acting.

5. Your employees know when things are going badly. They are closer to the job than you are. There is no need to state the obvious: "We're running behind; let's get going!" They expect you to work alongside them to plot a course through the maze the project has become. They are looking to your intellect and your intuitive sense of what will and will not work.

6. Intuition also tells you when to act and when to wait. Pressing ahead when employees or peers have con-

flicting opinions might yield temporary gains but will create future problems. Heartbeats provide a wonderful way to determine—to *feel*—the right moment to act. Before issuing orders pause for a few heartbeats—seven or eight seconds—to sense what is occurring in the room. Ask yourself, "Am I dealing with emotions and egos rather than facts?"

7. If you conclude that reaching agreement is unlikely, you have two choices. If time permits, suggest meeting later when emotions have cooled. If time is short, tell the group you realize a difficult task can make opponents of coworkers who care for one another. Then lead them back to their customary respect for each other by raising those points on which they would typically agree. After a few yes responses, the team will be less adversarial and more open to consensus.

8. Employees know the tyranny of numbers and realize your job and theirs depend upon meeting those numbers. But they expect you to value them as human beings, to know something of their personal lives without prying, to see them as more than performers. That means if you ask an employee how he or she is feeling and the response is "OK, I guess," don't nod and walk away. Say, "What do you mean 'OK'? Come on, let's talk." This small act reveals to employees you are a caring manager, someone they can trust and want to follow.

9. Ernest (and you) will succeed only by marrying the science of facts with the art of leadership. Employees assume you would not have been promoted without a

keen intellect, a superior track record, a powerful work ethic, and the appropriate technical expertise. But they will judge for themselves your level of respect for them. Do you listen to and value their ideas? Do you bring their achievements to the attention of senior management? Do you encourage them to post for higher openings and gain the skills such positions require? Can you convert conflict between associates into accord? Do you support them when they are criticized by other managers?

If Ernest (and you) find this balance between technical competence and human awareness, you can lead employees to achievements even the most ambitious data could never have predicted.

WHEN EMOTIONS OVERCOME REASON

Why Is My Boss Suddenly Angry at Me?

Overlooks What's Important

What You See

Felicia B., Executive Assistant, trade association

I told my boss the truth, and now I'm in trouble. This association does important work for our industry, and I love my job. But I think I jeopardized my career when my boss asked me why I was inquiring about our tuition refund program. I told him I was considering law school because a law degree would make me even more useful to the organization.

He looked so alarmed that I quickly reassured him I would be going only three nights a week and would confine homework and studying to evenings and weekends. I told him I wouldn't let anything cut into my work and that two of my friends are in the second year of the same program and their bosses aren't even aware they're in law school.

Looking back I should have kept my mouth shut because yesterday my boss gave me a poor performance review after a history of outstanding evaluations. I was so stunned by his comments that all I managed to blurt out was that I thought my work was as good as, or better than, ever.

We've always had a kind of father-daughter relationship, and his mentoring has changed my life, but since our talk he ignores me. If law school doesn't interfere with my work, why is he suddenly so angry? He wouldn't have a clue I was in school if I hadn't asked Human Resources about a tuition refund.

What Your Boss Sees

Arthur M., Trade Association President

An executive assistant at this association has got to be on call at all hours. Our West Coast members think nothing of calling my home late at night if they see a threat to their business and need us to lobby Congress. First thing next morning I meet with our legislative staff and schedule a visit to the Hill that same day. That's what members expect for their dues.

If Felicia is in class or studying, she won't be able to return to the office to assemble the materials we need to bring with us. Her loyalty has to be here, not to another career. Her work has begun to slip, and she isn't even enrolled. What will happen when she's deluged with homework? Our staff lawyers tell me they barely had time to sleep when they were in law school, and they weren't working! I don't see how Felicia can do this job and go to law school at the same time. She's going to have to make a choice.

MY DIAGNOSIS

Felicia has aspirations and has earned the right to achieve them. She's convinced she can continue performing at a high level while attending law school. Arthur also has aspirations, and a potentially distracted Felicia puts them in jeopardy. Her intention is perfectly reasonable: do my job and attend law school to advance myself. It's what ambitious people do, and her friends have proven it can be done. But if she wishes to keep her job while attending law school, she must first win Arthur's support.

The request she considers reasonable has collided with Arthur's emotions, his fear that law school will make her less attentive to him. In Arthur's eyes, Felicia is irreplaceable and his needs are more important than her ambition. Every one of us has experienced this clash when our seemingly plausible request is greeted with a blistering rejection. We're told no for reasons that bewilder us.

Perhaps anticipating her future as a lawyer, Felicia presented her case logically. "If not for the tuition refund you wouldn't know I was in law school." She presumed Arthur would respond with equal objectivity. But he hears only that law school will take precedence over him. Suddenly, despite Felicia's reassurances, his interests no longer will come first.

She describes her relationship with Arthur as father-daughter, and fathers have mixed feelings when daughters bring home the man they plan to marry. Suddenly, someone else has become more important. Arthur ignores the merit in Felicia's decision, hearing only that he's being displaced by law school. She fails to see that what is perfectly sensible to her is emotionally unacceptable to her boss.

Felicia must look beyond reason to convince Arthur that her commitment to him remains as strong as ever. Here are actions to take when the slightest possibility exists that someone's emotions can overcome your logic, when your reasonable request is greeted with a shocking "No!"

ACTIONS I RECOMMEND

1. Experience should have warned Felicia that Arthur counted on her availability, that any intrusion would upset him. She should have realized she was initiating a discussion bound to be far more complicated and personal than a simple request to attend law school. Arthur is more likely to approve law school if convinced Felicia is not abandoning him—a difficult task, but not impossible.

2. When an innocent remark unleashes an outburst, do not become defensive. Accept immediately that this discussion has shifted from objective to emotional. Remain silent for a moment, asking yourself why you have hit a nerve. Resist the temptation to provide more facts. They carry little weight in this discussion. Feelings suddenly have become more important than reason. Instead, consider asking, "Have I done something wrong? Is there something I don't understand?"

3. Quickly acknowledging that something unintended in your comments caused offense could prevent positions from hardening. The responder might even realize he or she overreacted. Being alert to the impact your words are having on someone will quickly tell you if additional facts are needed or if you are being asked for something deeper, your understanding of the other person's feelings.

4. There comes that moment in everyone's career when it is time to ask the boss for help: "Marketing has created a new opening. It's a job I'd love to do and know I can. Will you put in a word for me?" You consider this a perfectly understandable request. You are ambitious and see an opportunity to benefit the organization and further your career.

Before asking for such help, put yourself in your boss's place. You are complicating his or her life—replacing a proven performer with someone untested. Could your leaving signal to others that Marketing is a faster lane to advancement than your current department or that your boss is not developing you? Ask yourself how you would respond if you were across the desk.

It would help if you could explain that you have identified a replacement who could absorb your duties seamlessly. Suggest that, once in Marketing, you could foster more productive alliances with your current department. Who at higher levels should hear how much you've learned from your boss, and how do you convey that? Never forget that while you are thinking of your career your boss is far more concerned with his or her own. You must help your boss see that the two are not in conflict.

5. Be sensitive to those subjects likely to evoke emotion in the listener. Felicia knows Arthur well enough to have predicted that her request would trouble him. She should have gone to him before exploring the tuition refund, reaffirming her commitment and suggesting that law school, on a restricted schedule, could enhance her value to the association, and to Arthur.

This would cast Arthur in a familiar role, that of mentor to his young assistant. It would have acknowledged his influence on her life. Instead of seeking guidance, Felicia surprised her boss with something she had decided on her own, implying a change in their relationship, a change Arthur resented. Approached for his counsel, he is far more likely to appreciate Felicia's aspirations and even assume his traditional role of helping her achieve them. Presented with a decision, however, he thought only of the threat to his own primacy.

6. In her discussion with Arthur, Felicia must assure him that his guidance nurtured her career, that the wisdom he imparted is now being expressed through her work. Without the confidence he helped instill in her, she could never have contemplated law school.

7. Arthur must hear that he helped inspire Felicia's dreams and that he remains profoundly important to her. He will undoubtedly feel some sense of loss as she becomes more independent. But if reassured that he has not lost her loyalty, Arthur is far more likely to see her determination to go to law school as a victory for both of them.

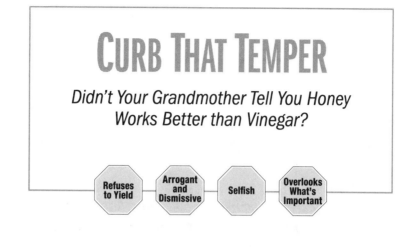

CURB THAT TEMPER

Didn't Your Grandmother Tell You Honey Works Better than Vinegar?

Refuses to Yield — Arrogant and Dismissive — Selfish — Overlooks What's Important

What You See

Alexandra B., Interior Designer, design firm

Three of my kitchens have been in Architectural Digest, *and I have more Palm Beach and Beverly Hills clients than anyone at this firm. The president knows how much business I've won for her and encourages my work and rewards me well. My problem is with a few clueless clients and with designers who resent me because my work gets attention and theirs does not.*

Our fabric buyer just had a wedding shower, and I heard about it only when my coworkers returned, lugging gifts and laughing. I don't care if they dislike me, but I hate that they help each other at deadlines yet leave knowing I'll be here until midnight completing drawings. Also, two of my clients have been spending time at the board of another designer. If she tries to steal them, she'll hear from me.

What Your Boss Sees

Sharon K., President

*A*lexandra *has a sense of space, color, and light unmatched by anyone I've ever hired. Our firm has always had A-list clients, but she's brought in their daughters. Yet, for all her talent, several of our clients and most of our staff refuse to work with her. She rolls her eyes when a client insists on changes and has a shrill temper that erupts without warning.*

Several times I've had to intervene in shouting matches between her and other designers, and I once had to snatch the phone from Alexandra as she argued with a client. I pretended she had just gotten bad news from home and asked the client to forgive her. One of the young clients she brought in—a lawyer—wants Alexandra to do her new apartment but insists that I join them when they can't reach agreement. She loves Alexandra's taste but says she has enough battles in court and doesn't need them when choosing pillows. I shudder to think what I'd do without Alexandra, but she's not bigger than the firm. We did well before she came and will do well if she has to leave.

MY DIAGNOSIS

*E*ven allowing for artistic temperament, employees are expected to show respect for associates, clients, and their employer's values. The most accomplished performer will not be tolerated very long if his or her behavior is disruptive. Alexandra is a gifted designer; even associates who dislike her acknowledge her talent. But they won't work with her. Clients who hired the firm for her services are beginning to shield themselves from her.

As gifted as she is, Alexandra's behavior must change if she is to remain with the firm. Instead of erupting when her suggestions are rejected, she must learn to move gradually from mild dissent to respectful disagreement.

I frequently hear complaints about managers who seem to have no middle ground in their responses, who leap unpredictably from mild irritation to anger. Associates, especially subordinates, become fearful of saying or doing anything that might trigger rage that erupts without warning. Opinions are expressed tentatively, if at all.

There are ways Alexandra (and you) can make certain to control that temper.

ACTIONS I RECOMMEND

1. The best way I know to control my temper is found in the martial arts. Students of karate, judo, and similar disciplines don't act abruptly. If, for example, we were seated opposite one another and you unknowingly began kicking me, assuming you were tapping the table leg, I would back away as far as possible. If you continued, I would quietly say, "You don't realize it, but you're accidentally kicking my leg." If you continued, I would gradually escalate my response, but I would never begin by reacting sharply. This technique would benefit Alexandra, whose sudden leap from impatience to anger is costing her clients and collegial support.

2. Alexandra will win client approval and peer support if she expresses design ideas passionately, not condescendingly. If the client is cool to her concept, Alexandra could patiently illustrate the play of color and space to draw the client into the plan so vividly apparent to her. If, instead, Alexandra becomes frustrated and insistent, the client will only withdraw further. The "Oh, I see what you mean!" moment is achieved only through collaboration, never impatience.

3. If a client is dismissing my ideas and frustration grips me, I turn to my martial arts training and step back from an exchange going nowhere. I am not the important element in this equation. My attention becomes riveted on the person who *does* matter, the client who is expressing little interest in my idea. That person and his or her convictions will determine the outcome of this exchange, not my insistence.

4. It is my task—not the client's—to ask myself, "Why am I not reaching them? How do I enlist them in something so visible to me?" I certainly don't do it by pressing more aggressively, as Alexandra often does.

5. Rather than becoming impatient, I find it best to ask the client, "I thought I had a solution, but you don't agree. Is there something I'm missing?" I'm the one who has to hear what a client really wants, not the client who must hear me. Often, our differences can be resolved if I make subtle changes in the approach we've been discussing. If our differences are significant, I discard my suggestion and listen even more carefully to the client. Ultimately, it's her organization, and she

knows it far better than I do. The client is rejecting my plan, not rejecting me. We start fresh, working to find a solution as partners, not opponents.

6. Alexandra will convert the client into an opponent if she sees any hesitancy as a rejection not only of her ideas, but of her as a designer. The client's right to disagree will become a personal affront only Alexandra perceives, igniting both her temper and a clash she cannot win.

7. Alexandra must never forget that it is the client who will live in the completed space. Convincing the client to accept something he or she will soon regret is not a victory for Alexandra. She only wins when the client loves the design, feeling it has emerged from the collaboration of two people on the same quest. That collaboration calls for an intimate partnership, not a flashing temper.

Sharon wants Alexandra to remain with the firm, her talent is too precious to lose. Alexandra will have more of her work in *Architectural Digest,* if she looks inward before responding and asks herself, "Am I overreacting to a rejection only I feel?"

DON'T MANAGE THROUGH INTIMIDATION

Be a Boss, Not a Bully

Selfish	Arrogant and Dismissive	Refuses to Yield

What You See

Anthony McG., Vice President, Agency Relations, insurance company

My job is to keep our agents happy; they generate the premiums that pay our salaries. People here at corporate say they respect the agents, but they really don't. Otherwise they wouldn't be looking for ways to cut commissions or the trips agents work so hard to win. Agency managers are competitive, and they'll drive their people all year to win a golf outing at Pebble Beach. Without a powerful agency force, this fancy building would be empty.

A corporate bean counter has just announced that our upcoming sales meeting is too expensive, that fewer people should qualify to go to a less-expensive resort. Agency managers have heard the rumor and have come to me for help. I won't let them down.

What Your Boss Sees

Vernon S., Senior Vice President, Field Operations

Tony has all the tools to be the best advocate an agency manager could have. He defends their interests and helps corporate types understand the pressures agents face. He was one of our best producers for twelve years before he agreed to come to the home office. I expected Tony to be the perfect liaison between the field and home office, but he intimidates people and isn't winning their support. He's smart and knows what goes into selling a policy, but he is so relentless he can wear you down. That relentlessness combined with his size—he played football at Penn State—cause people to avoid confronting him. They either go around him to get things done or complain to me. My boss asked me just yesterday if Tony would be happier back in the field.

MY DIAGNOSIS

Self-assured people with a depth of knowledge—especially if physically imposing—can be intimidating. The most confident associate with a compelling viewpoint will wilt when an exchange with such a figure becomes heated. I've seen participants say they agree when it's clear they remain unconvinced. A relentless coworker is easier to walk away from than to reason with. More receptive listeners can be found elsewhere in the building.

If, like Tony, you combine knowledge, zeal, and a forceful demeanor, people might agree with you simply to end the discussion. Rather than attempting to convince you, they will simply nod and leave. You assume you've pre-vailed only to later find they've ignored you.

Your knowledge, dedication, and assertiveness can make you a valued advocate, one whose requests typically win approval, rather than an intimidator whose interests are dismissed.

ACTIONS I RECOMMEND

1. If associates often withhold their support from you, ask yourself why. You want only what's best for the orga-nization, why don't they see that? Look at yourself as others might. Ask a trusted associate to tell you how he would feel if you were trying to convince him.

When advancing a project is your face taut, are you leaning forward, or is your voice edged with impa-tience? If so, relax your features, lean back, soften your tone, and let others speak without interruption. You've done this before when talking with someone you admire or care for. Recapture that feeling when you're meeting resistance, and go forward more gently.

2. Don't lose sight of your primary goal. In Tony's case it's to be an advocate for the field, making certain that agents loom large in every corporate decision. His tone could obscure that goal, making it appear to others that his real objective is to dominate them. So they ignore him and those whose cause he's advocating.

An intimidating figure barging ahead might feel potent but is really ineffectual. Associates bypass such a person, rejecting the same request they would welcome from someone less combative. Tony will lose his corporate pulpit if he doesn't remember that agents want him to win support for them, not alienate those who can provide that support. Achieving goals, not menacing others, is the real measure of Tony's (and your) effectiveness.

3. Tony would be a far better advocate for agents if he acknowledged that in a troubled economy a sales meeting must not appear extravagant. Just a few concessions would reassure the accountants they are being heard. Not having an open bar, making gratuities a personal expense, limiting the duration of the meeting, and traveling coach rather than business class might please corporate staff and save Pebble Beach. It's up to Tony to decide what's more important to him, bullying the bean counters or saving the trip.

4. It is also important to know how to respond to managers who are attempting to bully you. My work frequently brings me into the presence of those who have honed intimidation into a weapon. Their tone makes it clear that I have only seconds to earn their respect or be dismissed. While dealing with such a business buccaneer I can feel myself shrinking into my chair as the bully looms over me.

   At the moment I think the chair is about to swallow me, I reach deep into myself to find something of which I am very proud, something the intimidator never experienced. For me it was being an eighteen-year-old member of the 101st Airborne Division. The pride I feel, the respect I earned long ago from men more impressive than this intimidator, comes out and the nature of the meeting changes.

I have passed some arcane test. It is nothing I say, and I certainly don't move threateningly. Something in my manner—perhaps in my eyes—makes clear that I deserve the same respect I accord the would-be bully, and he or she sees it.

When you sense someone is attempting to intimidate you, look inward to find the achievement of which you are most proud. It can be an academic honor you've earned, a race you've won, a skill you've mastered, the family you're raising, or the pride you take in your career. Something from within will transmit itself, making clear that you will not be intimidated.

5. Bullying bosses inspire fear, not allegiance. They fracture rather than build teams. They barge ahead, never realizing that no one is following them. The finest leaders I know have a gentleness about them. There is steel inside, of course, but they don't feel the need to flaunt it. Tony (and you) must realize that people avoid bullies, knowing there is nothing admirable within them, only a noisy, hollow space.

PART 3

Behavior That Keeps You Stuck

"We won't tolerate behavior like that in this organization" is something I often hear when a manager acts in ways associates find both puzzling and offensive. "They had to know what they did was unacceptable here. What were they thinking?"

Innocent missteps are excused and quickly forgotten; everyone slips occasionally. But if your lapses are frequent and appear intentional, you will soon erode trust throughout the organization. Violating its unwritten code of behavior will cost you the support of associates and probably your promotion, perhaps even your job.

I've taken the following case studies from many workplaces to illustrate how to avoid behavior that keeps you stuck.

WHAT IS URGENT AND WHAT CAN WAIT

Know What Is Air and What Is Food

Doesn't Delegate   Rigidly Analytical   Overlooks What's Important

What You See

Greg M., Founder and President, direct marketing firm

When the corporation I worked for went bankrupt, I vowed never again to work for anyone else. I spent eleven years running every level of a direct mail business and decided to use my reputation and contacts to start my own company. Things are picking up, but the stress is getting to me. I spend twelve hours a day here but am always behind. I don't sleep worrying about things I've left undone. Every morning I'm greeted by new problems and never get to my priorities. I don't want to go back to a large company that could collapse under me, but maybe I'm not cut out to be my own boss.

What Your Boss Sees

Michael J., retired company president and advisor to Greg

I've been trying to help Greg; he worked for me years ago and affectionately calls me "Boss." He's learning what every fledgling entrepreneur quickly discovers: being an owner is very different from being an employee. He no longer has the resources he enjoyed in corporate life—assistants, support departments, the latest technical advances, or associates who could jump in and help in an emergency. Now the buck stops with him.

Greg must stop putting out fires and focus on the challenges that will make or break his company. Above all, he must satisfy existing clients and win new ones. Instead he's overwhelmed by problems that must be dealt with but can wait. I'm afraid if Greg doesn't focus on priorities, he'll be back working for someone else.

MY DIAGNOSIS

What once was considered job-hopping is now commonplace. Résumés that would have been discarded just a few years ago reveal the human side of job elimination, bankruptcies, mergers, and outsourcing. Employers understand it's now the norm for applicants to have held several jobs within a few years. This turbulence has created a cohort of highly competent men and women determined to start their own businesses rather than seek employment that might be short-lived.

The new entrepreneur accustomed to corporate life must quickly learn that everything begins and ends with him or her. Rarely can the actions of one employee put a company at risk, but a business owner has that power. Failure to know what is urgent and what can wait can be lethal.

I've served as a resource to the Young Presidents' Organization, an association of men and women who became company presidents before age forty. Members are wildly diverse—Ph.D. and high-school dropout; scientist and telemarketer; female and male; black, white, Hispanic, and Asian; introvert and backslapper. But all are laser-focused on what cannot wait. They ignore everything but their goals and what must be done to attain them. They rush from bankers in the morning to union organizers at night, without losing sight of the critical event at each meeting. What isn't destructive to their businesses can wait.

The following suggestions will help whether you wish to start your own business or run your department with entrepreneurial fervor.

ACTIONS I RECOMMEND

1. A company, like the human body, has vital signs that measure its health. Doctors check your pulse, blood pressure, and heart rhythm for indicators they consider vital. Customers also assess your vital signs: Are your products or services better than your competitors'? Do you deliver on time? Are your prices reasonable? Are you quickly responsive to requests and complaints? Do you create new ideas and services that help your customers stay ahead of *their* competitors? Make certain

you know your company's vital signs. Take a coldly analytical look to assure they meet or exceed your customers' expectations.

2. Greg must learn that paying bills, renting space, buying furniture, leasing computers, and interviewing prospective employees are important tasks but not critical. They can be deferred, left for weekends or evenings.

3. The difference between important and critical is the difference between food and air. You can survive long periods without food. You die quickly without air. Greg (and you) must learn what is air and what is not before customers go elsewhere.

    The endless administrative tasks confronting Greg are important, but they are food, not air. Satisfying existing clients, winning new ones, exploiting your competitive advantage, anticipating change and responding to it, and assuring commitments are honored *are* air.

4. Just a few years ago business friendships made allowances for slightly higher prices and the occasional mishap. An embarrassed apology during lunch soothed any distress. But that's no longer true. Relationships are a distant second to the impersonal bottom line. Yes, customers want you to provide service that demonstrates your personal involvement. But an increasingly unforgiving marketplace has little patience for old boys doing business over drinks.

5. To succeed amidst intense competition, you must show customers two disparate strengths. First they must see that their business is important to you personally, that you hold yourself accountable for satisfying them. "This is my company, and I'm here for you. I answer the phone, not someone in India." Prospective customers will find your personal commitment appealing since so many business contacts have become distant and unfeeling, as in "All representatives are now helping other customers. Press one to remain on hold."

Once customers sense your commitment, a second strength becomes paramount. From the very outset you must deliver high-quality products or services on time, at the right price. "But I'm just starting out" will win no sympathy from disappointed customers or clients.

6. Desperate to succeed, you'll find it hard to turn away anyone who wants to buy what you sell. When I started my consulting firm, the word *no* disappeared from my vocabulary.

But I never forgot that I depended upon referrals— satisfied clients telling others I was worth a try. Even in the global marketplace, people who know you bump into one another. One unhappy customer or client, voicing dissatisfaction, can dash your dreams.

7. You must be a fresh alternative to larger, long-established firms. Otherwise why should a client take a risk on you?

Focus on the vital signs of your venture. Blend the art of personal service with obsessive attention to detail and you'll build the company of your dreams. If you do, you will never have to work for anyone else again.

But if you do choose to work for someone else, run your department as though it were your company. I took that advice myself years ago. Like many employees in large organizations, I often felt anonymous, that my ideas would never filter through the levels above me. That changed when I overheard a passing manager complain that customers in certain zip codes rarely paid their telephone bills on time. The comment remained with me, and that weekend I drove to two of those neighborhoods and asked people passing by if they would speak to me about their telephone bills. A surprisingly large number did—all of them complaining that the bills were too complex and contained too many unexplained charges.

Over the weekend I prepared a report suggesting ways to make bills more understandable. My boss said my recommendations were impractical, but somehow my report reached a senior vice president who appointed me to a task force that had been reviewing the billing process. Suddenly I was no longer anonymous.

I encourage you to think and behave like an entrepreneur. It's exciting, and your boss will notice.

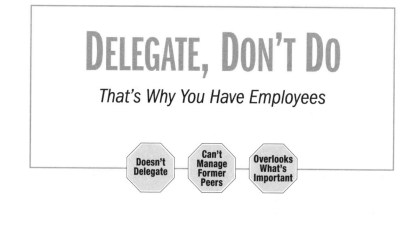

DELEGATE, DON'T DO

That's Why You Have Employees

Doesn't Delegate · Can't Manage Former Peers · Overlooks What's Important

---

What You See

Beth B., Store Manager, national retailer

I've risen through the ranks, from trainee to junior buyer to sales manager to group manager and finally this, my dream job, store manager. While I'm told I'm responsible for this store and its $60 million in sales, I'm visited regularly by Merchandising, Human Resources, and Operations vice presidents who give me conflicting orders. One tells me to be out on the floor pushing associates to generate more sales. Another criticizes me for demanding too much of my people, telling me that Human Resources is getting complaints about me. Someone else insists I've got too many salespeople in women's shoes, one of my hottest departments.

I've just gotten my new budget, and we're expected to do 10 percent more in sales with six fewer associates. Oh, yes, and I'm to provide more floor space for handbags, hold two trunk shows, and then have a cooking demonstration while we're taking spring inventory!

My latest performance review had lots of "Satisfactory" ratings and very few "Exceeds Expectations," and I'm working twelve hours a day, including weekends. My fiancé complains he never sees me, while my boss says she expects more from me than I'm already giving. I came to this store flying, but I'm beginning to wonder if I can do the job without killing myself.

What Your Boss Sees

Antonia N., Regional Vice President, Merchandising

Beth has all the tools to be a successful store manager. She has design flair and is good with people. The buyers love her openness to new styles, and, unlike most merchants, she doesn't fight the Operations people who control expenses. When I recommended promoting her, I assumed she'd quickly become one of our top store managers. Instead she's lagging behind peers with far less potential. She's becoming a "doer," not the leader I expected. My boss wants to visit Beth's store, and that's usually the first step to demotion. I'll protect her for a while, but she's got to get her arms around the job, and quickly.

MY DIAGNOSIS

I was asked to mentor Beth and found her eager for coaching. I suggested I shadow her as she attacked the avalanche of tasks that fall upon a store manager. She led me out of her office, explaining she began her day by walking the floor to assess staffing, housekeeping, and the pulse of the store. We were not five feet from her office when a harried employee carrying an armful of dresses rushed over and said, "These have been marked down, but I'm not sure where they belong." The store manager looked at a few tags and said, "Put them on the couch in my office. I'll get to them when I return."

Moments later, with the office still in sight, another associate hurried over, saying, "Operations wants us to cut two people in bedding, and we have a sale beginning Saturday. How am I supposed to sell without people?" Beth paused and said, "I'll be back in an hour. Meet me in my office, and we'll figure out something."

These were just the first of many interruptions that trailed us as we walked through the store. Common to every exchange was Beth accepting tasks that should have remained with subordinates. They came running to her with a problem and left unburdened and relieved.

Her failure to manage her store was evident in these brief exchanges. "You've taken on about six hours' work and we've just started out," I told her. "If you limit yourself to the problems you've just accepted, you'll have little time for anything else. Let's go back to your office and talk."

Time management is a book in itself, but these simple steps will help Beth get everything done and still have time to think and plan. And it's thinking that pays her salary, not doing the work of others.

ACTIONS I RECOMMEND

1. Most managers presume they can do every job better than their subordinates. But the successful ones
quickly realize they must delegate if they are to meet
their goals. I told Beth that all employees who came to
her shared the same objective, to dump their problem
on her. Instead of demanding a solution, she absolved
them of responsibility. They were at home enjoying
dinner while she was sorting out their problems.

2. Managers must delegate. That's why you have employees. Clearly state your expectations and have them
repeated to assure they are understood. ("Take a second
to tell me what you hear me asking of you.") Monitor
periodically to measure progress. Reward or discipline
based on that progress.

3. Stop being more concerned about your employees'
workloads than your own. Avoid guilt feelings, which
prompt you to assume their responsibilities. As busy as
they are, you are busier. Most employees will tell you
when your expectations are unrealistic. Until they do,
hold them accountable for jobs they must complete.

4. Require employees to come to you with solutions rather
than problems. Talk through their proposals, encouraging, suggesting, and refining as employees shape their
solutions. Then hold them accountable for what they
have proposed. Being required to think and accept
responsibility for their recommendations will help
them grow. Developing employees, rather than doing

their work for them, is what a manager does, and it's what you must do if you and they are to advance.

5. It is tempting for a manager to succumb to employees' entreaties and do their work, thinking "I can do it faster myself." You must pause and ask yourself, "I know they're working hard and this is a tough one, but am I doing them a favor by relieving them of responsibility?" The answer most often is no. You are helping a subordinate remain a subordinate.

6. One poor performer can deflate an entire department, while a dozen productive employees rarely can elevate a mediocre peer. When evaluating employees, most managers immediately begin discussing their poorest performer, describing at length the fruitless meetings they've held with them. Weaker employees often resemble leaky tires—you add air, but they quickly go flat.

Meanwhile your best and brightest feel taken for granted. If given a fraction of the time lavished on those who produce little, your key employees would soar to still higher levels. Of course Beth (and you) must devote time to marginal employees, but not at the expense of those who quickly convert mentoring into improved results.

7. Your most productive employees lose respect for you if you tolerate those whose work must be absorbed by others. Provide counseling and progressive discipline until experience tells you that you've gone far enough. Then act.

Facing imminent demotion, Beth hurriedly incorporated these suggestions into managing her store. She became more demanding of her staff, developing them into partners in the store's success rather than bearers of problems. In the words of her boss, she has "finally gotten her arms around the store. Beth has become the manager we thought she'd be when we promoted her."

Just one thought on time management. In the past when I received any written material—a letter, report, invoice, bank statement, or publication—it seemed to become part of my hand. I'd read it, place it on a pile, reread it, shuffle it to another pile, and read it once more before finishing with it. I was uncomfortable sending a reply, for example, that hadn't been thoroughly edited. I found myself pondering the smallest word. When receiving e-mails "Keep as New" became my default site.

Eventually it struck me that I was being paid to make things happen, not be a clerk or editor. Today, if a document doesn't require detailed review I read and respond swiftly. Moments after it arrives, it is gone. My replies might not win literary awards, but they get the job done. I do the same with virtually everything that reaches me, touching it just once, leaving me time to think and plan.

If you find yourself losing ground to the flood of material you receive, think about touching everything just once and making "Send Now" your default response. It made a major difference for me.

FINDING SANCTUARY AT WORK

Keeping Your Job While Forgetting Pain, if only for a Moment

Overlooks
What's
Important

What You See

Bimala R., Customer Service Manager, furniture wholesaler

When my father died I had no choice but to take my mother in. She has her own apartment on the lower level of our house with a full bathroom and small kitchen. We planned to rent the apartment for some badly needed income, but now it's Mom's. She's not easy and sometimes makes me feel like a child again with her criticism of my cooking, my housekeeping, and the way I raise my children. My house no longer feels like my own. Worst of all, she resents my leaving her to go to work and frequently calls me there for no reason.

What Your Boss Sees

Alejandro L., Vice President, Sales

I've been grooming Bimala since I first interviewed her. She lit up the room—bright, assertive, customer-sensitive, and ambitious. Her husband has a pretty good job, but she's the main breadwinner and eager to advance. Until last year she was on a fast track, and I could see her taking my job in a couple of years. But her entire disposition has changed. She's become distracted and moody, often leaves work early, and is on the phone with personal calls. Her last performance review shook her, and I saw some improvement for a while. But she's still not the old Bimala. Forget about getting ready for my job, she isn't doing her own.

MY DIAGNOSIS

Every day I meet employees who have watched their children leave home only to find their parents have arrived. They receive calls at work they haven't gotten since their children entered kindergarten. "I've got to get home because my mother . . ." is heard frequently as aging parents are forced to leave their homes elsewhere to be nearer their children.

Others come to work with their own anxieties: chronically ill children, ailing spouses, single parenting, a failing marriage, or money worries. Medical advances extending the lives of the aged and the desperately ill and high divorce rates combine to place a heavy burden on those who come to work wondering when the phone will ring.

Like Bimala, these employees must care for parents, children, or spouses, taking time and attention away from work. Bosses, not immune to such concerns, will be patient—for a while. But that patience wears thin, and an employee's absences and loss of focus are increasingly resented. Missed assignments are completed by others or left undone. However caring a boss is, he or she will soon begin wondering if balancing work and home has become too much for the employee.

Failing at work leaves an employee with no place to be safe, no sanctuary. Home is worry-filled, and pain follows him or her to work. There is no place to heal, to be free of anguish. Bimala is desperate, knowing neither her mother nor her boss is pleased with her. She (and you and I) can still succeed at work by leaving pain at the office door, if only for moments at a time.

ACTIONS I RECOMMEND

1. Recently my cell phone rang as I waited at the airport to be met by a client's Human Resources manager. It was my wife telling me that one of our daughters was being admitted for emergency surgery. The manager drove up just as I told my wife I'd be on the next flight to our daughter's home.

I raced to the ticket counter only to learn the earliest flight on any airline departed in four hours. I told the manager that I'd remain at the airport awaiting the flight. She surprised me by saying, "Bob, you've told me and others in the company that when there's trouble at home, work can be your sanctuary. You said you can lose yourself at least temporarily by immersing yourself in work. Take your own advice and come to the office for your meetings. We'll get you back in plenty of time."

I did and for a few minutes at a time didn't agonize over my daughter's surgery. My family and I gathered that evening at the University of North Carolina Medical Center to learn my daughter would be fine, and, thank God, she is.

I took advice I'd given to many employees: find sanctuary at work when problems mount at home. You must have refuge somewhere, and you're not finding it at home. You're also putting your job at risk by letting anguish pull your mind from work to home. Even the most compassionate boss will not allow your lingering distress to threaten the department. Your focus and effectiveness are drifting, and your boss sees it. Losing your job will leave you with no place to heal.

2. The president of the company where I was working is a parent and was deeply moved by my pain. But his empathy is not boundless, and he expected me to conduct productive meetings. This took an act of will, a strength I didn't know I had, but both he and I benefitted from my plunge into the assignment. Sitting alone at the airport would have left me with nothing to do but worry. Work gave me moments of relief, and his managers learned.

3. Make work your safe place, your sanctuary. Lose yourself for moments at a time by concentrating on work.

However agonizing your personal life, you'll be startled to find time passing as the job distracts you, and it will.

4. Should you sense one of your associates is bowing under the weight of distress carried from home, help her find sanctuary at work. You will be doing that coworker a kindness and perhaps saving her job.

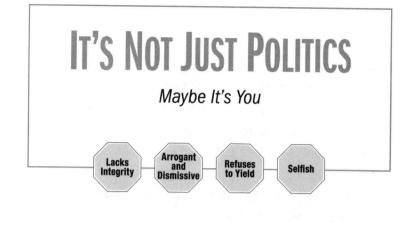

IT'S NOT JUST POLITICS

Maybe It's You

Lacks Integrity | Arrogant and Dismissive | Refuses to Yield | Selfish

What You See

Diane L., Investment Banker, financial services group

This place reeks of the "old boys' network," and I'm not a boy. Deals that should come to me—I speak fluent Japanese—go to people who wouldn't know *sayonara* from *bonjour*, yet they're on their way first-class to Tokyo. I've confronted my boss about this, and he mouths nonsense about Asian male chauvinism and tries to placate me with minor deals in Cleveland. I'm as experienced and tough as the guys he favors, and I'm better educated. But around here it's not ability that counts, it's politics.

What Your Boss Sees

Vernon C., Managing Partner, international banking

Diane joined us from one of the most aggressive firms on Wall Street and brought her combativeness with her. When-

ever she's frustrated—and it's often—she'll sing her old firm's praises. I've often felt like saying, "If they're so good, go back!"

We're tough and will go head-to-head with anyone for business we want. But we don't treat junior staff condescendingly, aren't arrogant, and don't bad-mouth or undercut members of the firm to steal their clients. Diane does that and more. Some of our clients love her, but others, especially those in Asia, find her insensitive and even crude.

She accuses them of disliking assertive women, but it's not that at all. Several have women in key positions but are uncomfortable with Diane. Why can't she understand that rampant aggressiveness is unacceptable here? If she doesn't change she'll either continue handling second-tier business or be out.

MY DIAGNOSIS

The glass ceiling, which pressed down on generations of women, has lifted dramatically in recent years. Corporate dining rooms that once admitted women only on Secretary's Day now are alive with feminine voices. In many companies, however, women are still held to stricter standards, especially in careers they've entered relatively recently, such as engineering, manufacturing, construction, and investment banking.

Were she named Dan, Diane would likely be viewed as a hard-charger who needs some—but not too much—reining in. Her "rampant aggressiveness" would be viewed as admirable competitiveness. But she is Diane, and, however unfair, she is judged differently than a man.

Diane's frustration must be redirected into behavior her associates find constructive if she's to win that Tokyo assignment. Above all, she must understand that her firm's unwritten rules of behavior are as indelible as Securities and Exchange Commission regulations.

ACTIONS I RECOMMEND

1. Joining a new organization is no different than entering the home of a stranger. You must quickly become aware of what is acceptable and what is not. A few missteps can mark you as an intruder. Seek out associates who are welcoming. Ask them which senior executives want you to call on them and those who expect you to wait until summoned. How are expense accounts prepared and submitted? Are some charges frowned upon? Learn the unwritten protocol of meetings: Where do you sit? May you bring coffee? Do you wait a meeting or two before voicing an opinion? How much debate is tolerated?

2. As you develop trusting relationships, you can ask if there are associates who resent your coming, if your first steps are being viewed favorably or not, and if there are subtle rules of conduct you are violating. Diane should ask if her assertiveness has crossed the line into combativeness. Hopefully, someone will tell her that praising your old firm never wins friends.

3. Learning and honoring an organization's expectations does not mean being submissive. You are avoiding mistakes and the time wasted to correct them so you can concentrate on doing your job. Unwritten norms might appear to have little to do with the job, but your awareness of them tells your new associates a great deal about you.

4. Diane must accept that while the glass ceiling is ascending, women are still judged more critically than men in virtually every organization I go to. Forceful men are viewed as setting high standards, but the same behavior in a woman is regarded as strident or worse. Women enter new organizations bearing a burden men do not. Like men, they must quickly prove their value. Unlike men, they must pay far greater attention to where perceptions blur. At what point does setting high expectations become being unreasonably demanding? Where does confidence become arrogance, taking initiative not being a team player? These are questions Diane must pose to herself and to a few trusted colleagues.

5. Diane and other women face a twofold challenge. They must do what every manager does, make things happen. But they must do so knowing their behavior is subject to greater scrutiny than a man's. Any violation of an organization's norms is quickly noted. Attitudes about gender certainly have softened, but skepticism of women as leaders remains alive in many executive suites I go to. Women are still held to more demanding standards. That's why I feel safer when a woman captains the plane I'm on.

6. Strong-willed women like Diane have an even tougher choice to make. She can continue to blame "politics" for her failure to progress, or she can do some soul-searching and find that point at which her actions and ambition converge with the firm's rules of behavior. If she chooses to look inward, Diane will soon be on a plane to Tokyo.

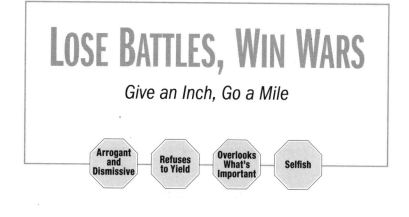

LOSE BATTLES, WIN WARS

Give an Inch, Go a Mile

Arrogant and Dismissive — **Refuses to Yield** — **Overlooks What's Important** — **Selfish**

What You See

Ramesh W., Vice President, Distribution,

supplier of medical equipment

They hired me to convert this company's shipping and receiving procedures from manual to computerized. I spent ten years automating the distribution centers of one of the country's largest retailers and could do this job blindfolded. Our customers demanded that we tie our logistics into theirs and ship only when their system tells us to. They told us that if we didn't reduce their inventory they would find a supplier that would. Millions of dollars of business could be lost if we don't automate. That's why I was supposed to have free rein in reengineering our systems.

Yet, every program I install is opposed by our people. I knew the union would fight automation that reduced head count. But even more resistant to change are the very managers who interviewed and hired me. They don't realize that computers and not *hourly employees must control the movement of cartons if we're to satisfy hospital administrators desperate to cut costs.*

What Your Boss Sees

Edgar L., Senior Vice President, Logistics

We recruited Ramesh from a retailer that gets products from supplier to customer faster than anyone in the world. He's great at what he does but has made so many enemies so quickly that I'm afraid people will fight his ideas just because they're his.

Our union's business agent is tough but realizes that if we don't automate to cut costs and improve efficiencies none of us will have jobs. He'll negotiate fairly if we treat him and his people with respect. But Ramesh fights him on every little point, never giving an inch. Every union demand is dismissed as impractical. The business agent gets his back up and blocks changes he privately admits make sense.

It's not just the union. Ramesh treats every concern associates raise as a rejection of his ideas. When other managers express the slightest doubt, he says they're clinging to the past. Why can't he see that people are threatened by change even when they know it's inevitable? He could win our cooperation and the union's if only he evaluated our ideas and adopted those that could work within the new system. We must automate, but I'm not sure Ramesh's the one to do it.

MY DIAGNOSIS

When a routine call to our bank is answered in India we know the world has changed. Change troubles most of us, especially when it threatens our livelihood. We will tolerate, even welcome, change only if confident that those rearranging our lives are doing so to our benefit. The most receptive of us will resist change if we sense we are being manipulated, that the trash on the floor is our career.

While I think I've convinced myself that I welcome change, I can respond to the unexpected by hunkering down. I recently was asked to speak to managers about fostering change at a company I've visited many times. As I approached their headquarters along a familiar road, I was confronted by a man waving a stop sign. "The road is closed," he called out. "You have to turn around."

I pointed to the complex behind him and insisted that he could see I was almost there. He patiently replied that going farther was impossible. I told him a roomful of people were waiting for me and that I'd be late if he didn't let me pass. He remained as calm as I was frustrated and said, "Sir, you'll sink in the asphalt. Just turn around and take the service road behind you. You'll be there in three minutes."

I turned, drove to the meeting, and said to those eager to hear my wisdom, "Let me tell you how this expert just dealt with change." I've never again been impatient with people resistant to change.

ACTIONS I RECOMMEND

1. Before initiating change, remember that the systems you are altering were designed by the very people whose cooperation you need. They must not be made to feel they or their ideas are relics.

2. Without losing your sense of urgency, enlist as many associates as possible in shaping the new systems, encouraging and employing their ideas wherever appropriate. Tell senior management how valuable their support has been. Such collaboration takes time, but moments invested now will spare you months of passive resistance and frustration.

3. Be willing to concede on minor matters even when convinced you are right. I have seen projects grind to a halt when egos clashed over issues that, in the long run, proved meaningless. Step back from the heated exchange and ask, "Is this something I can accommodate on so we can move ahead?"

Stepping back from a clash of egos is especially difficult for men. Many see yielding on even the most trivial issue as a test of their manhood. Yet, the most self-assured men I work with are willing to accommodate if doing so achieves the larger purpose. They know the difference between accommodation and compromise. Accommodating is the willingness to accept modifications that don't alter the character of a project. Compromising means violating one's principles, one's sense of right and wrong. One is acceptable, the other not.

4. Ramesh must find ways to win the trust of the union's business agent. Together they can convince union members that without automation and the transfer of high-volume, low-margin products overseas the company will lose business to price-cutting competitors and that jobs surely will follow. Well before painful decisions must be made, assure employees that you will involve them in decisions affecting their lives. Once you have earned the trust of union members, their willingness to make sacrifices will astound you. Should you lose that trust, the ferocity of their resistance will be equally astounding.

I recently watched as managers in two different factories announced that the assembly lines employees were gathered around were being transferred to China. In one plant the news evoked fury. Cat feces were heaped into drums containing raw materials. Operating instructions were shredded. Critical machine parts were unbolted and taken from the plant. Tools and dies painstakingly refined through the years were hammered into scrap.

Twelve miles away, in a plant owned by the same company, machinery was improved even as it was being packed in crates with Chinese ideograms. Helpful notes were appended to operating manuals. Parts being placed in shipping containers were wrapped with care.

Why such radically different responses by members of the same union, employed minutes apart by the same company? In one plant, managers expressed their own pain, vowed to do everything in their power to attract new product lines from corporate, and, most important, had long involved employees at every level in developing new processes that would make the plant more competitive. Everyone was aware—albeit unhappily—that for the company to survive some machines that had provided employees' livelihood for decades had to be shipped abroad.

Plant supervisors and hourly employees had put aside historical differences and became unified in their determination to make it unprofitable for corporate to transfer even more product lines. Together, they sought new ways to do old jobs, increase productivity, and develop products so sophisticated they could not be entrusted to plants six weeks away by ship.

In the plant where the response was to sabotage rather than form a partnership, decisions were made in closed offices. Convinced employees would halt production if told some lines were being transferred, managers never took them into their confidence. Drivers making deliveries to the plant became the main communications source, warning employees of manifests with Chinese characters. Employees who sought information—many of them with long service and willing to make sacrifices to keep their jobs—were told not to worry.

The plants had everything in common except trust. That trust has kept one plant open while senior management repaid the sabotage by closing the other.

Finally, Ramesh (and you) must never forget that what may seem like a logical response to global competition is for many the anguish of lost jobs. If Ramesh continues to innovate, but this time does so by enlisting employees at every level in his quest, he will find support from those he formerly considered enemies.

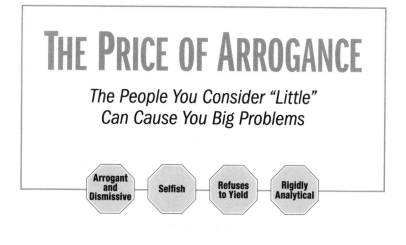

THE PRICE OF ARROGANCE

The People You Consider "Little" Can Cause You Big Problems

Arrogant and Dismissive · Selfish · Refuses to Yield · Rigidly Analytical

---

What You See

C., Jian, Senior Vice President, Marketing, pharmaceutical company

I accepted this job for one reason, to become president when the CEO retires in five years. They recruited me because of my experience in India and China, crucial markets for this company. At first I had clear sailing, developing new customers and suppliers and winning praise from the president and board. My boss met frequently with me, supporting my decisions and offering, but never pushing, advice. Lately, however, our meetings are different, not as cordial or personal. I don't know what's going on, but something is, and it doesn't feel good.

What Your Boss Sees

Stuart B., President and CEO

Jian was a bonanza for us, a young Columbia-trained biologist with extensive sales and marketing experience in countries we had difficulty entering. He got off to a flying start, winning customers and suppliers in India and China who previously regarded us as too small to bother with. But a number of our dedicated, long-service employees are saying Jian is very difficult to work with, that he's cold, abrupt, and concerned solely with his own advancement.

I anticipated that a younger executive with new ways of doing things would upset some of our people and discounted their early comments. I was convinced they would accept him once they saw he was protecting their jobs by making us an important presence in India and the Far East. But recently our Human Resources director told me that some of our most valued young scientists and managers say they will leave if Jian is in our succession plan. They complain he dismisses their recommendations and barely acknowledges their contributions at the few meetings he does bother to attend. This got my attention because virtually all of them were thrilled when Jian first brought his unique experience to us.

We need Jian, but I can't let this company lose what has made us special—a top-to-bottom respect for people. Yes, we have a generous benefits and bonus program, but our employees care about us because we care about them.

Every manager in the company holds frequent, informal meetings with employees at all levels, sometimes just to say "Thank you." Some of our most profitable products have come from ideas generated deep within the organization. A woman *who joined us fresh out of a community college just completed her doctorate in pharmacology through our tuition refund program and was named a vice president in our research facility. Jian was the rare exception to our standard policy of promoting from within. I want him to become the leader our people will follow, but they will not accept him if they find him condescending or unapproachable.*

MY DIAGNOSIS

Employees may no longer expect the care "Ma Bell" and similar companies lavished on their people years ago, but they do expect to be treated with dignity and respect. Younger employees, especially, are quick to revoke their loyalty if they sense they are regarded as interchangeable parts.

Jian was hired to revitalize the enterprise by instilling a global vision, and he quickly proved he could do just that. Already an experienced researcher and marketing manager, he realized his ideas would meet resistance when they collided with the old. But flush with early success, he made little effort to build relationships with coworkers beneath the CEO and board. He assumed his alliances at the very top were enough.

Support at the top can be fleeting if complaints bubble up from disaffected employees. Your halo will quickly tarnish if company leaders hear morale is declining and that you might not be the savior they thought they had hired. Jian is about to learn that those who lead companies take morale very seriously and will not put their enterprises in the hands of those who ignore the culture they have fostered.

Recently I was asked to meet with the vice chairman of one of the country's largest retailers who had been hired as eventual successor to the CEO. Within months complaints about his remoteness and autocratic behavior began reaching the president and board. At first, key board members urged patience, suggesting that his initiatives would gradually win respect. But even they became troubled after hearing that some of the company's least judgmental, most respected staff members were avoiding the heir apparent, meeting with him only when they had no choice.

The vice chairman met with me as reluctantly as an aristocrat would a commoner. Several times during our lengthy meeting, I went to a sideboard for refreshments, always bringing him coffee, juice, and snacks. He rose just once, returning with water for himself. I asked why he didn't inquire if I wanted something. He seemed oblivious and then puzzled, as though wondering "Why would I do that?"

His self-absorption was so total that I decided to risk a question I felt confident he couldn't answer. "What's your secretary's name?" I asked. "Sheila," he replied. "No," I persisted, "her last name." He didn't know. Nor did he know if she was single or married or had children or not. She had worked for him for eight months and was of no more interest to him than the desk at which she sat.

Following my report on the meeting, the CEO and board agreed the vice chairman should leave. He had everything they originally saw in him except humanity. Jian is fast earning that same reputation.

ACTIONS I RECOMMEND

1. If those in your new company conclude you are being groomed for senior management, perhaps eventually the presidency, your every act will be scrutinized. Even before you learn where the bathroom is, hold a meeting with your direct reports, emphasizing that you need their advice and support. Let them hear your admiration for what they have worked so hard to build.

2. Quickly hold meetings deep within the organization where uncertainty about you is interfering with work. Employees are asking: Who is this new person? Will his own team be coming too? Will she shake things up before she knows anything about us? And, at the heart of their concerns is the question: Is my job safe?

3. In these meetings avoid bravado and recounting personal successes. Tell enough to convey a picture of who you are and the vision you bring; then emphasize your respect for the enterprise you are honored to join. Those seeing you for the first time will hear your words, but your behavior will tell them who you are. They will approve modesty but cringe at pomposity. They will leave the room with an impression of you that will take months to alter. Make certain that initial opinion is "the new person seems OK."

4. Do not make sweeping personnel changes until you have assessed the effectiveness of those reporting to you. Judge their performances under your leadership. Do not accept the opinions of others unless they coincide with what you're seeing for yourself.

5. Quickly learn something about each of the people working with you. Will their personal situations require some flexibility from you: a single parent, family illness, or physical handicap? Also know their attainments and comment on them: a gifted child, a notable spouse, community leadership, athletic or scholarly prowess—anything of which they are proud. They must sense you care about them as individuals and not as assets. Your note celebrating an achievement an employee didn't realize you were aware of will be taped to the refrigerator.

6. Have lunch periodically with employees, attend occasional office celebrations, and walk throughout the building exchanging greetings and ideas. The few moments spent in such informality will be discussed for hours by employees at all levels.

7. Lavish praise publicly, taking little or none for yourself. Your team will repay you with even greater performance. Senior management and the board will also take note of your strong, but modest leadership.

　　For all his potential, I fear Jian will squander this opportunity if he doesn't implement these suggestions and shed his disdain for others. He (and you) must rein in self-assurance that borders on arrogance. Let others see for themselves the strength and competence beneath your quiet confidence. They will want you to be the leader of their department or organization.

CONFRONTATION ISN'T A DIRTY WORD

You Can Be Both Direct and Respectful

Lacks Passion for Change · **Doesn't Delegate** · **Old Boys' Club Mentality**

What You See

Rebecca S., R.N., Night Nursing Supervisor, metropolitan hospital

I'm called a nursing supervisor, but my real job is trying to get aides to do the work of L.P.N.s and R.N.s. We've had so many staff reductions that every nurse who wasn't let go is now supervising people who have little experience or training. Whenever I bump into another R.N. or L.P.N., we share horror stories about incorrect medications, intravenous drips not flowing, patients not fed or bathed, and dressings not changed—errors that rarely occurred when the hospital was staffed by professionals.

I understand we don't have the budget to hire skilled nurses, but staff and attending physicians expect the same level of service we provided ten years ago. They and department heads constantly complain about errors that my people make. How can I expect poorly paid aides to perform duties that weren't part of *their training? I went through a four-year degree program; they have had two years of schooling or less and some barely speak English. I can only hope they'll do their best and somehow get the job done.*

What Your Boss Sees

Kanesha F., Director of Nursing

Rebecca is a good, old-fashioned nurse, the kind diploma schools turned out a generation ago. She is a dedicated professional, and I'm fortunate to have her on my staff. But she doesn't realize how completely this community has changed and that we're now an inner-city hospital starved for funds, not the shiny medical center she entered in 1990.

Her people aren't as strong as she or I would like, but neither are they as weak as she thinks. A more demanding supervisor would hold them accountable for lapses and demonstrate how to do the job properly. A strong leader would set realistic, but high, expectations. Lazy practices wouldn't be tolerated as "they're doing the best they can." Her staff's limited training and accents give Rebecca an excuse to exempt them from doing a professional job. But some of my most no-nonsense L.P.N.s and R.N.s rave about the performance of aides no different than hers.

I know most of Rebecca's staff want to perform at a high level. Several were nurses in their countries and are working toward certification here. I see their faces when a patient is ignored; they're embarrassed and know they could have done better. All they really need is a supervisor who expects more of them than Rebecca does.

MY DIAGNOSIS

Every day I meet managers at all levels—from first-level supervisor to CEO—who are reluctant to confront subordinates who aren't meeting expectations. It's as though *confrontation* is a dirty word and that setting rigorous standards and insisting employees meet them is too much to expect of today's workforce. Rebecca requires less of her people, and they respond to those expectations. They know she views them as quasi-professionals who aren't trained to meet high standards. Everyone's expectations dwindle—Rebecca's, her staff's, and their patients'.

Too often employees being terminated for poor performance exclaim, "But nobody ever told me!" and a glance at past annual reviews supports them. Rarely is there documentation other than "Meets Expectations." The act of telling someone they're underperforming becomes—for many managers—a personal intrusion too uncomfortable to bear.

Some feel that confrontation could trigger conflict, and so they avoid it. The employee either stumbles unwittingly toward failure or meets the low expectations set for him or her. This penalizes both employee and enterprise. Rebecca (and you) must never be reluctant to confront marginal performers.

ACTIONS I RECOMMEND

1. Malingerers aside, most employees want to do a good job. They cherish your confidence when you give them the toughest challenges. You wouldn't assign those tasks if you didn't respect their competence and work ethic. Countless experiments have proven that randomly selected employees held to high expectations outperform those from whom little is anticipated.

Young men and women become better just putting on the Marine Corps uniform because it implies that much is expected of them. You elicit pride when you tell employees you reserve the tough assignments for them. Rebecca does the opposite: she imparts a sense that mediocrity is tolerated, even expected. Don't demean your employees by requiring so little of them.

2. *Confrontation* is not a dirty word. In its barest essence, it is looking directly at employees and telling them the truth about their performance. Of course you impart criticism thoughtfully, knowing that your words will almost certainly embarrass and upset your employees when hearing their performance must improve.

3. Speak to employees as you want to be spoken to, respectfully and without overstatement, and offer a course of action leading to improvement. The discussion is blunt but instructive and laden with hope. Obviously, a discussion prior to termination—when all alternatives have been exhausted—is different. It is still respectful, but sad, because both of you have failed.

4. Even the most conflict-averse manager can effectively confront an underperforming employee by saying, "This assignment isn't going well. Is there something *I'm* doing or not doing that's getting in the way?" You

are pointing at yourself, not the employee, making it difficult for him or her to become defensive.

The employee might reply that you've provided too little information too late. Assure him or her that won't happen again. Provide any missing material, making certain the employee is now equipped to do the job. Then say, "This must be completed no later than noon on Friday." That's direct and respectful confrontation.

5. It is vital that you see no contradiction between enlightened management and holding employees to high performance. Every old soldier or athlete fondly remembers the drill instructor or coach who demanded more, saw potential, and insisted he or she fulfill it. Conversely, there is little nostalgia for superiors who regard us as ordinary and ask for little.

6. When I was a young soldier, my first sergeant caught me goofing off and said he was disappointed in me. It's a memory I still carry. His respect was something I cherished then and still do now. No criticism has ever struck me harder. He expected more of me than I was giving. I let both of us down. I vowed never again to expect less of myself or of those who work with me.

7. Rebecca (and you) must have confidence that senior management knows the difference between high standards and abusiveness. Employees want you to elicit the best that's in them. They lose respect for you and for themselves when you accept mediocre work. They expect you to confront them forthrightly when they are not fulfilling their potential.

Rebecca's staff might not consist of L.P.N.s or R.N.s, but they will provide the highest level of patient care if she treats them as professionals—confronting them when they fall short and praising them when they meet high expectations. Your employees are no different.

YOU CAN BALANCE FAMILY AND WORK

But Make Certain Your Boss Doesn't Resent Your Family Time

Overlooks What's Important

What You See

Jack N., Associate, corporate law firm

Like every associate, my goal is to be named a partner. I just heard I'm on the list of those being considered and am flattered. This firm attracts graduates from the country's best law schools and demands that we produce an enormous volume of high-quality work during the endless hours we put in. Making partner is the reward for all that effort.

My particular expertise is insurance law, and the senior partner I work most closely with represents many of the country's largest financial services firms. His number is speed-dialed when insurance companies or banks face a potentially serious problem or contemplate an acquisition. Richard had his choice of the best associates here, and he chose me. Without his backing I wouldn't be a candidate for partner.

What Your Boss Sees

Richard G., Senior Partner

Jack is an outstanding associate and has spared me hours of work, particularly in researching cases and precedents that go back to the Depression. He is more than a hard worker; he has a creative intellect. He's suggested approaches to threatened financial assets that I'd expect only from someone with far more experience. I was delighted to recommend him for partnership.

Partnership decisions here must be unanimous. One dissent is enough to drop you from consideration. I was convinced Jack would have no trouble and went to the nominating meeting confident I would be giving him good news.

I was shocked when two of my partners rejected Jack. I immediately demanded to know why, insisting he was exactly the kind of younger partner we needed. Both gave the same response: he's at family events when he should be in the office. I couldn't believe what I was hearing and said so.

Our managing partner said he had summoned Jack on two separate occasions only to be told he was at his daughter's soccer match. Our senior litigator said that Jack had been at a son's play when he needed him. Both partners are older men and often reminisce about the hours they spent poring over documents when their children were growing up. With pride they say, "My wife's job was the kids; mine was the firm."

I work sixty-hour weeks but manage to get to most of my kids' events. Jack does the same and has never once been late with an assignment. But, I'm only twelve years older than he is, not thirty-five years older like my two partners, and I see things differently. They're in their mid-sixties but show no signs of retir-

*ing. Jack's got to satisfy them if he wants to make partner. I
would be violating my own beliefs if I told him to spend less time
with his kids and more at the office. I have to help him find a
way to do both.*

MY DIAGNOSIS

Male bosses in their late fifties or older rarely had the
luxury to balance family and work. It was expected
that they would spend the hours and endure the family
absences the job demanded. Like Richard's partners, they
left family matters to their wives as they ascended the
career ladder. Some are resentful, even jealous, of the close
family ties enjoyed by younger male subordinates, especially when reminded by their own children of important
moments missed when work called.

Jack has stirred these emotions in two senior men,
and his partnership has been delayed, perhaps lost. He,
Richard, and men of their generation frequently declare,
"My dad was too busy working to watch my Little League
games, and I vowed never to make that mistake." These
younger men—armed with the latest technology—insist,
"I spend plenty of time at the office, bring work home,
and am on my BlackBerry, cell phone, or computer when
the kids are asleep. I get the job done without being an
absentee father."

They do get the job done, but the resentment they
arouse in older men can obscure that fact. I often hear
older managers complain, "I go to his office when something unexpected blows up only to find he's at a kid's

swim meet or class play. That's great for his children, but I need him and so do the people who work for him. He's their leader and must be available to them. Do you think I wanted to spend Saturdays in Omaha playing golf with clients! I went because the job required it. Maybe he doesn't want this job badly enough." The emotion in those words can end a career.

Richard is right. If Jack is to win that coveted promotion, he must find a way to balance his roles as husband, father, and law partner.

ACTIONS I RECOMMEND

1. Being both parent and manager means attending enough of the play or game to please your children without offending your boss. I happily squeezed into my child's seat during "Daddy Comes to Kindergarten" but knew my boss was impatiently awaiting my return. Other fathers toured the school after we left the classroom. I ran for the train. With four children to support, I wasn't going to test my boss's patience or trigger his envy, especially since he had a son to whom he didn't speak.

2. I attended virtually all of my son's Little League games but arrived during the fourth inning. I saw my daughters' matches, recitals, and plays but checked the program to learn when they would perform. I knew that seeing every inning or every act would anger my boss. I struggled to find a balance that reassured my child and my boss that each was very important to me.

3. Talk to your boss during a quiet moment and explain you are committed to your job, that you would never leave for a family event without being in control of your assignments. During that discussion remember that your boss might never have forgiven himself for missing terribly important family occasions. Your words are passing through that filter. Say nothing to make your boss feel you are a better spouse or parent. Explain that your respect for your boss and for the enterprise would never allow you to jeopardize your work. You are simply trying to be both the best parent and best manager you can be.

4. Many senior managers are at a very different place in life than you are. They might unwittingly be making demands on you that they would modify if you asked them to. One of my early bosses was a childless New Yorker who routinely assembled his staff at 5 P.M. to review the day. As the meeting continued I could envision the 5:40 P.M. commuter train departing and then the 6:10 P.M. I could also see my wife coping with three children under age four wondering when I'd be home to rescue her.

   After another of these meetings, I asked my boss if we could start at 4 P.M. instead of 5 P.M. and told him why. While he couldn't begin to imagine the chaos at my house, he could see the tension on my face and agreed. Talk to your boss; he or she might be more understanding than you think.

5. Of course there are times when work disrupts family plans. This occurred often enough that my wife and I began passing each other, barely speaking, when I

returned home late. After a long talk, we agreed to have a Thursday night date, a romantic evening for just the two of us. It has become so central to our marriage that we would never consider missing one. (My travel agent frequently says, "It's Thursday so I made sure to get you an earlier flight home.") You might find such dates will enrich your marriage as you cope with a demanding job.

6. There is a test that will tell you how well you manage parenting and work. If you can listen without a hint of guilt to the absent father's lament when Harry Chapin sings "Cat's in the Cradle" you've done something right. You've achieved balance in two very demanding worlds. Hopefully Jack will make partner *and* be able to smile when he hears that song.

PART 4

Overcoming Bias Directed at You

Work, and the way it is done, has undergone a revolution since I began consulting. Companies in countries described as primitive not long ago now outperform iconic corporations. Businesses flourish in homes and dorm rooms. Technology that filled a room now fits in the hand. Teleconferencing is the civilized alternative to air travel. Five people in factories I go to produce more than fifty employees did in 2000. Layers of management have simply disappeared. Employees are expected to absorb the work of associates who once sat at those empty desks. College graduates who anticipated recruiters would compete for their services now are job hunting. Your heart misses a beat when you hear the entire staff is being summoned to a meeting.

But unchanged throughout has been the intimacy of my work, the trusting relationships established with those I mentor. We talk about disappointments, fears, hopes, and achievements.

Increasingly, something ominous has entered these discussions. While a harsh economy wounds everyone, its impact is especially hard on the minorities, women, and older employees I meet with. After listening to the experiences of at least seventy such employees at all levels, I felt obligated to add the following section on the unique problems they face at work every day.

RACISM REAWAKENING IN THE WORKPLACE

Black Is Still More than Just a Color

What You See

Earl M., Senior Vice President,
Domestic Marketing, search engine provider

just learned that I'm not replacing my boss as executive vice president of Marketing when he retires at year-end. He's been talking to me about his plans to retire, so when he unexpectedly came to my office I expected to hear that I was succeeding him. After five minutes of small talk he said, "Earl, this isn't easy, but they're bringing Rashid in from India to head Marketing. I told them you were my choice, but I'm halfway out the door and they ignored me."

It was as though he had punched me in the stomach. Louis has given me nothing but outstanding reviews since I've been here and routinely involves me in decisions that convinced me I was destined to succeed him. He might be leaving, but he helped build this company and if he really wanted me to head

Marketing, our CEO and board would have gone along. Rashid is good, but his experience is limited to India and the Far East while I'm responsible for U.S. sales, which generate nearly two-thirds of our revenue.

I can be blunt with Louis and told him I wasn't going to just let this happen. I earned this promotion and intend to fight for it. He told me that I'd only hurt myself if I went charging upstairs. He said I had a job others would kill for and shouldn't risk losing it. He told me I'd be getting more money and wider authority because Rashid needed me.

I've never before played the race card, but I told Louis the only reason I was being passed over was that I was one of the very few higher ranking blacks in a company run by whites and the few Asians and East Indians beginning to join them. Many of my peers met at MIT or Cal Tech. They see themselves as a kind of elite global brotherhood. I have a degree in electrical engineering from Purdue and can hold my own technically with any of them. But they've formed a fraternity I don't belong to. I'm certain that's why Rashid is in and I'm not. Race card or not, I told Louis I intended to see our CEO.

What Your Boss Sees

Louis F., Executive Vice President, Worldwide Marketing

Earl is in the right job; to promote him would be to set him up for failure. I've given him every chance to succeed me, but he doesn't have the relationships or status needed to command respect from people we're now doing business with. Most of our revenue is generated in the States, but within two years that will change. We're becoming a major player in China and India, which is why Rashid is the right choice. Earl does fine in this country, where IT managers and purchasing agents select vendors. He knows them, and they know him. But he'd be dealing with very different people in India and the Middle and Far East, where our market share is growing.

Earl won't be at ease among officials who speak three or four languages and are accustomed to having people cater to them. He'd be lost in that society. Rashid has degrees from India Institute of Technology and MIT and is the son of one of India's wealthiest industrialists. He grew up in the same world as those with the power to order their government agencies and corporations to install our systems. Earl was raised in a Chicago housing project and would not be comfortable in a private club in Shanghai, Riyadh, or New Delhi. I'd be hurting the company and Earl if I threw him into that world. If he makes a fuss upstairs he could lose his job, because we're not choosing him over Rashid.

MY DIAGNOSIS

The overt racism that crushed the hopes of Earl's parents is a distant memory in today's workplace. Earl attended schools his father couldn't have aspired to and made his way to the upper reaches of one of America's most admired companies. But Earl's generation faces its own barriers. A declining economy, with blue-collar and white-collar jobs flooding offshore, has created a vacuum draining away managerial positions.

As associates vie for fewer openings, I find competitiveness emerging even within managerial teams that consider themselves tightly bound. Some of this competitiveness is beginning to assume a racial tone. For the first time since African-Americans became a growing managerial presence in the 1970s, long-dormant racial concerns are reemerging.

Both black managers and white managers have begun telling me they worry that the other enjoys an advantage based on race alone. White employees once again confide that "they're not likely to terminate the department's only black underwriter; so I'm at risk even though I've been here longer."

Conversely, every African-American I know is convinced no congressman who shouted "you lie" to a white U.S. president would find his campaign account swollen with donations from across the country. Many African-Americans I speak with suspect some of their associates harbor resentments of their own against blacks, especially as competition intensifies. If someone can prosper after calling the president of the United States a liar, they question how associates would view an African-American ascending to the top of their company.

The racial remarks I hear today are far less strident than the resentment, contempt, and anger expressed when blacks began entering management in more than token numbers. A white associate who today would mutter any of the old insults would draw disdainful glares from coworkers and probably be disciplined. Some might feel, but no one would openly declare, "She's on BPT" (black people's time) about a tardy employee. Or, "I spent fifteen years here before becoming a manager; he was just hired as my boss thanks to our diversity program." Or, "Two white men I interviewed for the job are more qualified, but she's black and I've been told to promote women and minorities."

The comments I hear today are infinitely more restrained and subtle. But they are ever-present reminders to African-Americans that black is more than just a color. Examples are the assumptions that Earl would be uncomfortable in an exclusive club in Shanghai or that black men are more adept at daily operations than at long-term strategy. Some senior officers tell me they hesitate putting an African-American in a job demanding a significant stretch. "If he fails," they say, "the board might not want me to demote him. I can't take that risk."

This next might be dismissed as trivial unless it happened to you. One of the most effective CEOs I work with enjoys assigning nicknames to his direct reports, awarding them with humor, and a message: "Einstein," "Facts Factory," "Results Man," "Superwoman," and "Blocking Back." "Blocking Back"—a black man—told me, "I graduated magna cum laude from Harvard, never played football, and weigh 165 pounds, so my nickname doesn't really fit. But it tells me how I'm viewed—he's successful and he's black, so let's think of him as a jock."

He would never protest to the CEO, who would likely laugh and insist it was nothing more than an affectionate way of building camaraderie. But "Blocking Back" would rather be called "Results Man," a name more accurately descriptive than the one he's been given. Also, complaining could make peers wonder if he enjoys being part of the team.

Senior management teams know they have only each other to count on as they battle the enemy the economy has become. Anyone entering the team must quickly prove he or she belongs. As in a combat infantry platoon, the first question asked about a replacement in a hard-pressed management team is "Will they fit in?" African-Americans I meet feel they are judged less likely than a white colleague to fit in an almost exclusively white management team.

Earl and other African-Americans can surmount the most subtle barriers standing between them and their highest aspirations.

ACTIONS I RECOMMEND

1. If you sense even the vaguest hint that you are regarded as tactical—an implementer—rather than strategic, assess the world in which your organization exists. Can you foresee any changes in society or in your marketplace that might affect the company? Go to where your services and products are sold, and observe the reactions of those who encounter them.

The shelves at Home Depot are stocked with products manufactured by one of my clients. I frequently watch as customers glance at one of their devices, pick it up, inspect it, and either buy it or put it back. That thirty-second event often yields a torrent of information when I inquire what prompted their choice. No decision means more to a company than what occurs at the point of sale. You have more at stake in that decision than an independent market researcher. Spend a few hours gleaning information where those transactions occur; your boss will find your report informative.

2. Bring together informal focus groups—friends and neighbors—and ask how they evaluate your organization. Pay particular attention to young people, whose assessment of your company will shape its future. Ask those you encounter at meetings, on planes, and on the treadmill how they view your organization and its products and services. People love to answer these questions, and their replies might startle you, opening new possibilities for you to pursue.

Put your observations into a written report, and ask permission to present your findings at an upcoming staff meeting. Surround your data with the personal comments people have made about your organization. This is compelling and important information and should prove illuminating to your associates and to your boss.

3. Develop the habit of looking at the horizon, at what appears to be taking shape just beyond what you can observe. Ask yourself how your organization is likely to be affected in various scenarios: What marketing opportunities would open if your older customers begin using social networking? What can be done if employee morale and productivity begin slipping as benefits are reduced and desks are left empty? How would your company be affected if Hispanics cross over to products they previously ignored? What would happen if the best and brightest began rejecting your organization's offers of employment even in a down economy?

What do these shifts mean for your organization, your department, and the way you manage? Pose questions that are both narrowly and broadly applicable to what you do. Try to answer them with the full breadth of your intellect and imagination. Develop and then circulate a plan of action emerging from your observations.

4. Become a more active observer of the changes taking place around you. Don't walk obliviously past unfolding events that will soon affect you and your job. Years ago I traveled frequently to Hawaii, staying at a five-star hotel selected by my client. The dining room at breakfast was always filled with large Japanese families—husband, wife, three children, grandparents, and nursemaid. I thought "Wow, at this hotel that's got to be a $200 breakfast! I couldn't afford that with my gang."

On a subsequent visit the dining room was half-filled. Japanese men were not entering the restaurant with families but were hurrying alone through the lobby carrying McDonald's bags. These were not $200 breakfasts! I called my client's president and told her what I was seeing and asked if something was happening in Japan. "How did you learn that?" she demanded. "We just got new numbers and our sales to the Japanese are off." The bags of fast food were emblematic of something far larger, something easy to miss if one walked unaware through life.

5. Be even more alert to small events that often are early warning signals to your organization of something broader and more ominous. Periodically put your observations and recommendations into a report. Ask that your boss distribute it to those at higher levels who might have an interest. This will help demonstrate that you are a strategic thinker, comfortable with visionary concepts and not simply one who executes the ideas of others.

6. Never forget that before you are considered for the senior management team at your organization or at one you hope to join, someone will ask, "Will you fit in?" That person won't ask you directly, of course, but he or she will ask others. Begin your interview by describing the results you've achieved. While people might already be familiar with those results, in a very subtle way help them become aware that you attained them through a diverse or largely white workforce.

Describe what they probably don't know about you, boards you are on, organizations in which you've held a leadership role, the schools you graduated from, the communities you've lived in. Slowly they will become aware that you must have been alone or one of very few minorities in most or all of these situations and that you are at ease in any society, and will be in theirs.

It is possible that despite their years of working together, Earl never confided to Louis how he managed to navigate his way successfully through worlds far more alien than any traveled by Rashid. Earl is partly to blame that Louis is more impressed with Rashid's history than with his. Earl took for granted that his boss was familiar with his life outside the office. Louis saw Earl in only one dimension, someone more at ease with purchasing agents than with urbane power brokers.

Do not presume your boss knows very much about you beyond work. You are not being immodest if you occasionally mention achievements that will enhance his or her estimation of you and of your potential. Earl should have, and so should you. Louis had far less contact with Rashid but imputes power to him because of his father, the schools he attended, and the access they give him to those who sign important contracts.

Louis does not appreciate that Earl has succeeded on merit alone, that he has made his way successfully from a Chicago ghetto to a corner office—a journey far more trying than one from Mumbai to MIT. Louis must also be aware that many in the private clubs which so impress him have only recently gained entrée and will have more in common with Earl than with Rashid.

It is not a race card Earl is playing when he meets with his CEO, but a statement of how much the world has changed and of Earl's ease in that world.

Earl is fortunate to have had the way blazed for him by black men and women who endured indignities unimaginable today. I attended meetings twenty years ago at a pharmaceutical company during which two black researchers had to remain silent as marketing people questioned including East St. Louis in the launch of a new drug. "Most of the people there are black. Will they take calls from interviewers? Do they have phones? How will we poll local doctors? We're certainly not going door-to-door."

Such behavior is unthinkable today, but racial barriers do exist or are reemerging as jobs become scarce. Biases run deep and are extremely difficult to counter. As you compete for promotion, think about how race is shaping decisions being made about you. Use that knowledge to preemptively dismiss any perception other than that you will outperform any competitor as you become the perfect fit for the management team.

THE WORKPLACE REMAINS TOUGHER FOR WOMEN

The Glass Ceiling Is Higher, but Still There

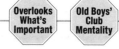

Overlooks What's Important   Old Boys' Club Mentality

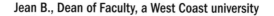

What You See

Jean B., Dean of Faculty, a West Coast university

Our provost has just been named president of a state university and will be leaving in June. I'm next in line and should
be replacing him, but a colleague warned me that other candidates—all of them men—are being interviewed off campus.
I refuse to think I could be passed over simply because I'm a
woman. I chose academia as a career because I wanted to
be judged not on gender but objectively on the degrees I had
earned, publications I had authored, and work I had done that
resulted in gains in the university's academic standing. I never
once felt being a woman has slowed my progress. It might even
have helped once the university became determined to make
the faculty and staff more diverse.

Universities are not cloistered monasteries; politics play a
huge role in one's advancement. I've moved ahead by chair-

ing committees, tutoring football players, hosting dinners for administrators and faculty, entertaining influential alumni, and presenting papers at professional conferences. I wouldn't have become dean of faculty if I had limited my activities to the classroom. The role of provost is a bigger and more complex job, but I'm ready for it and believe I've proven that.

What Your Boss Sees

Marcus T., University President

Jean was a great teacher and would have remained one if I hadn't encouraged her to become an administrator. She's a fine dean of faculty and has earned the respect of one of the best teaching staffs in the country.

But the provost must command respect for his or her managerial skills as well as for his or her intellect. This economy demands that I spend much of my time fund-raising. My provost has to be an assistant president, someone who runs the place when I'm away, builds consensus among schools and departments competing for funds, develops ties with important alumni and donors, and joins me at most board meetings. Jean has the academic pedigree the job requires, but I can't imagine her helping me manage an enterprise of this size.

If I don't promote her, I'll be vilified as antifeminist, but I've placed women, including Jean, in positions of authority across the campus. Our deans of law and architecture are women, two new board members are women, and the number of female department chairs has more than tripled on my watch.

But this is a university, and we do research. That research spotlights problems women continue to experience as senior managers. I'd need Jean to help me with salary negotiations and fund-raising, but one of the top graduate schools of business just completed a study that reveals problems she would face doing precisely that.

The study gave male and female managers the same script to follow in seeking reimbursement from a hotel at which their employer had just held a conference. Many rooms went unoccupied, and it was understood that the hotel would consider refunding the amount charged for those rooms.

Objective observers, tasked with the role of hotel financial officer, were asked to evaluate the performance of those seeking reimbursement. Almost unanimously the women—reading from the same script as men—were judged so "aggressive and offensive" that they were denied reimbursement. Virtually every man, on the other hand, was judged "courteous and competent" and given a full refund. It was inferred from the research that women generally would be far less likely than men to prevail in tense financial negotiations, especially in a troubled economy.

This and other current research conducted by business schools confirms that women managers continue to meet barriers not faced by their male counterparts. Ambitious young women are aware of those barriers, and many reject business careers. In our law and medical schools, as in universities across the country, more than half the students are female. Despite all our recruiting efforts, barely a third of the students in our graduate school of business are women, and that's also true nationwide.

Part of me wants to promote Jean. But with our endowment shrinking, our tuition already too high for most middle-class families, and the need to provide financial aid to more than half our students, we cannot afford to make fund-raising any more difficult than it already is. I can't risk having Jean seen by a *major donor as aggressive and offensive. We'll have to select from one of the superb male candidates available to us.*

MY DIAGNOSIS

The glass ceiling continues to rise dramatically, and women now hold managerial positions once reserved for men. But most of those gains have been achieved in lower and middle management. Women now account for more than half the nonagricultural workforce but fewer than one-fifth of corporate officers. Less than 2 percent of Fortune 500 CEOs are female. College-educated women are paid 89 percent of what men in comparable jobs earn, and it appears that gap has begun to widen.

Most women managers I work with have experienced these barriers but say they concern themselves less with bias than with finding the most effective way to balance family and career. "I've got to be perfect as wife, mother, and executive, and it's hard. People advise me to be less tough on myself, but the demands I place on myself got me this job and the life I have. I'm always asking other women executives how they get everything done."

Others say that to succeed they must suppress the very characteristics that make them a woman. "I managed to earn a Stanford M.B.A. and become a division manager without losing my instinct to be helpful, inclusive, caring, accommodating, and feminine. But the successful men around me—my competitors—are independent, impatient, forceful, and demanding. My boss has those traits and admires them. If I felt they'd make me a better manager I'd adopt them, but I get more from my team by being the person I am. My boss frequently refers to me as 'nice,' and I'm afraid that word could be my managerial epitaph if I don't behave more like a man."

Current business school research demonstrates that however she behaves, it remains extraordinarily difficult for a woman to win a reputation for being both competent and caring. In a noted study, male and female subjects received two telephone calls in rapid succession, one stating that a massive systems failure just struck their department and the other that their daughter had become ill.

Women who said they would elect to go home to care for their daughters were described by observers as incompetent. Those who said they would remain at work to oversee repair of the system were judged uncaring.

Men who chose to go home were described as caring, while those who said they would continue to work were called competent. One female subject said in exasperation, "We're damned if we do, damned if we don't!"

Certainly the workplace has become far more welcoming to women; success stories abound. But conscious and unconscious biases remain that can block a woman's rise to higher management. There are ways for women to become senior officers while remaining true to the people they are.

ACTIONS I RECOMMEND

1. Business school research reveals that women and men who have mentors receive more frequent pay increases than associates who are not mentored. But even when both are mentored, men are promoted at a far faster rate than women. The income of a mentored woman rises, but she ascends in rank far more slowly than the men around her.

A woman must be aware that the same mentor who encourages a male protégé to seize the next opportunity for promotion might warn her that being overly ambitious could get her labeled as aggressive. Appreciate that your mentor is trying to protect you, but don't let him or her restrain your determination to advance. Seek and pursue emerging opportunities.

2. One significant difference I find between male and female managers is that the moment an ambitious man is promoted, he begins preparing himself for the next step. Women, on the other hand, explore every nuance of the new job, spending far more time mastering it than a man would. He's ready for the next promotion while she remains immersed in her assignment. Learn the job, of course, but know when it's time to look upward. Men do.

3. Before initiating a new project, find an ally, someone who can take your side, especially at meetings with senior officers, and can remark, "No, that's not what I hear Jean saying. She just wants to make certain that. . . ." The very same words that would make you appear defensive are considered the objective assessment of a colleague who sees the merit of your argument. Men almost always have an associate willing to advance their causes. Women must find someone

ready to stand alongside them in the corporate clash of wills.

4. Before chairing an important meeting, hold individual discussions with all or most participants. Explain what you hope to accomplish and that you want a productive exchange of ideas, not a rehash of old arguments. Solicit ideas and expectations. Listen carefully to learn where conflict could emerge and who might or might not support you. Forceful voices can override the tightest agenda and take the meeting in a direction not chosen by you. Keep the agenda in your hands by identifying potential adversaries and advocates before the meeting begins.

My experience at dozens of meetings chaired by women convinces me that the first man to speak often gives or denies permission for other men to be combative, dismissive, or sarcastic to the woman at the head of the table. A widely respected man endorsing your opening remarks will help assure that the meeting does not become a thinly veiled debate about women in management. This in no way suggests that you need a man's validation. It remains your meeting, but there are times when a male ally can be useful, just as when marketing needs the support of manufacturing or when a man needs the backing of a female colleague.

5. It is often a struggle to be heard above louder, deeper voices when you are the only female in the room. A wise woman once told me that the noisier the room becomes, the more softly she speaks. Once the din recedes, she resumes her normal tone. "I learned," she said, "that when I raised my voice to be heard I sounded shrill. So, I began to speak softly, and gradually the room became quiet." The first time you try this will be a challenge. "Will they even hear me, or will they think I'm a terrified mouse?" If you are confident you've earned the right to be in the room and have a comment worth hearing, your quiet voice will command attention.

6. Women in senior management who are members of private clubs often find that the men they invite to lunch are presumed to be the members and that they are the guests. This is especially embarrassing when the male guest is given the menu containing prices or the bill to sign. Before your first meal, go to the club and make clear that you always want the proper menu and the bill. Don't leave this to an assistant; go in person. Don't undervalue the importance of belonging to a club. If offered membership, accept; if not, request it.

7. Current research indicates that women who advocate for themselves are less successful than women who advocate on behalf of a team or group. Men asking for a salary increase or perquisite for themselves are generally far more successful than women who make the same request. Think about this when you perceive that you are not receiving rewards you have earned. You are far more likely to prevail when you advocate on behalf of your department, employees, or management team.

This does not mean that you should shrink from insisting on what you have earned. But consider couching your request in these terms: "My department generates as much revenue as the others in our division. But neither I nor my direct reports earn as much as the managers in those departments. I'd like you to consider making an adjustment."

You might bridle at the prospect of not advocating for yourself. I'm suggesting that you do so in the manner most likely to succeed. Being assertive on behalf of a team yields far less opposition than being assertive for oneself, and it is far more likely to be successful.

8. The great challenge for women in management is to find that balance between caring and competent. Women I've worked with who have achieved this balance almost always have one highly developed skill that transcends gender. Examples that come immediately to mind are female chief financial officers, merchants, designers, and entrepreneurs. They are feminine *and* expert. One holds the door open for them but is quick to obey them.

I urge you to develop a skill that earns you a reputation for being both feminine and expert. This need not take years of reeducation. The world is changing so rapidly that opportunities you can master are surfacing every day.

A woman I work with decided to become a recognized authority on employee compensation. She achieved her goal by working relentlessly to learn everything possible about this complex subject. Soon she was no longer "a woman in Human Resources," but "the one who can take this mess and make it a credible policy." She began receiving calls from recruiters and invitations to conferences once closed to her. Think about how you can become the authority on a service or product offered by your organization.

9. If you are hired by another organization, ask that any announcement of your appointment be understated. When shown the announcements their new employers had released about them, several women I know exclaimed, "Wow, who is this woman! I've got to meet her." They were greeted at the door by the resentment of their new male colleagues. "After all our years of failing, we've found our savior! How did we become a leader in our industry without her?"

It took months for many of these women to overcome that resentment; some never did. Every misstep, however minor, prompted someone to proclaim, "Guess she's not perfect after all." A woman entering a senior role needs supporters, not vengeful men eager to help her fail.

Men arriving on a similar wave of praise can expect to be greeted with resentment, but I find the emotions awaiting women have a harsher bite. Ask that adjectives in the announcement describing you be toned down.

10. If an older male executive is among those interviewing you for a job, he might ask if you are married. If you reply that you are, he might inquire if you plan to have children or how you'll balance family and travel. Such questions are the stuff of Human Resources nightmares, but some older men continue to ask them. Resist the temptation to say, "You aren't allowed to ask me that!" You'll win the argument but lose the job. Just say, "I'll do everything the job requires and more."

But, as the song goes, "The times they are a-changin'." Chief executive officers who don't spend sleepless nights wondering if they have the right staff to meet those changes are putting their organizations in harm's way. I meet with teams assembled for safer times that execute strategic plans taking them backward. So confident are they that the economy will resume its familiar course that it's risky for a member to express doubt or suggest a new approach. You hesitate to speak up when others in the room regard your concerns or ideas with a smirk. Such teams are generally so similar in background, gender, race, and experience that thinking rarely strays from the familiar.

The few members who do have doubts groan that nothing will change until a few men retire, taking with them their influence over the shaping of ideas. They tell me they are grateful shareholders and employees aren't exposed to some of their meetings.

I feel a difference just walking into meetings with teams in other organizations. New approaches to the services and products that built the company are eagerly debated. "That could work" is heard rather than "It's not in our business plan." Exchanges are heated but respectful; no one voicing skepticism or an irreverent idea is made to feel stupid. Participants challenge the CEO.

Such teams even *look* different. There are women defending increased investments in their operating divisions, younger people proposing social networking as a marketing tool, and minorities reporting results in the Hispanic marketplace. No one is sitting back, sullenly mocking an associate's proposal. You realize that it's safe to dissent and be passionate about ideas, which, in other rooms, might end your career.

One of the major differences I find between these two types of teams is that women are either absent or minor figures in one and respected contributors in the other. In both, women still encounter conscious and unconscious biases not experienced by men. But economic shock waves have begun to erode the confidence of some of the boldest CEOs I know. Those who wouldn't waste a moment debating gender differences speak of something missing when they seek opposing points of view. One recently told me, "I leave meetings feeling we've only scratched the surface of possibilities open to us. Either people are afraid to challenge me, or we're too much alike. Maybe we need some new voices."

This uncertainty, this willingness to reshape leadership teams, provides the opportunity for women to make their way into senior management. Have the courage to tell your boss that viewpoints unexpressed at senior staff meetings are harming the organization. Explain that caring and competent women can help fill that void. This is the time!

YOU WANT TO RETIRE BUT HAVE TO WORK

Your 401(k) Is Now a 201(k)

Overlooks What's Important · **Lacks Passion for Change** · **Overstates Problems**

What You See

Lori M., Office Manager, steel mill

When I came to work here this was one of the largest steel mills in the country. We now occupy one small corner of the old plant and are owned by an investment bank in Chicago. Instead of bosses with callused hands, we get hurried visits from young people who wouldn't dream of dirtying their shoes on the mill floor. You could take pride in producing huge beams and sheets of steel that built this country. We now recycle cans into ingots that get sent to Korea, not something you brag about.

There are 110 of us left, not the thousands whose families worked here for generations, like my father, older brothers, and uncles. But it's a job, and I need it. When the big mill closed, my pension dropped to practically nothing. My husband had been laid off, and his union insurance policy turned out to be worth just $21,000 when he died last year.

Some of the bankers who come here look at me funny, as though I'm from another age and place. The few times they bother to talk to me, they ask why I still work. They say they'll retire before they're fifty. But I don't have shares in this place, and between my so-called 401(k) and pension I don't have enough to get through the next four years when I turn sixty-two.

I work hard, know everyone in the place, update all the personnel files, do all of the billing and most of the purchasing, deal with OSHA, and handle all the environmental paperwork that keeps us out of trouble with federal and state officials and tree huggers. I'm the one who makes sure all our records are current and that every fact and figure that leaves here is correct. I intend to keep working hard until I can afford to retire. All I need are four more years.

What Your Boss Sees

Reggie F., President and COO

I took Lori with me when the big mill closed and investors in Chicago approached me to run this boutique operation. There weren't many jobs for Michigan State metallurgists, and I grabbed it. I heard later that the other managers—most of them senior to me and more experienced—weren't considered because they were regarded as too old.

I've been getting pressure to terminate Lori because they think what she does can be computerized or handled at corporate. I've been able to protect her, explaining that state and local officials know her family and would rather deal with her than with an outsider. But she's beginning to make mistakes, not so much in her work but in things she says and does.

She keeps talking about the old days, when guys sweeping the mill floor made $35,000 a year and had great benefits. Lori is not old, but to a twenty-eight-year-old M.B.A. she can seem ancient and out of touch with technology. When they ask her to put data on a flash drive she says, "I wouldn't trust all this information to that little gimmick; I'll fax you hard copies." Paper to these people is like papyrus. They think it belongs in a museum.

She's got to stop saying and doing things that date her and make her look out of synch with people who thrive on technology. They're coming at me harder, claiming she's outdated overhead. I know her financial circumstances and am trying to save her, but they might start questioning whether my loyalty is to Lori or to the investors.

MY DIAGNOSIS

Reggie made a very important distinction when he said Lori is not old but can seem ancient because of things she says and does. Freshly minted M.B.A.s are contemptuous of those who lives aren't wrapped around a fiber-optic thread. Someone whose universe fits into his or her pocket can only seethe when Lori offers to fax material to them.

The past is of no interest to those who measure time in quarterly reports. To someone in kindergarten at the time, the pay of a steelworker twenty years ago is meaningless. Reggie can try to convince corporate visitors that Lori's work has value, but they will overrule him if she appears tied to the past.

Everyone viewed in today's workplace as older—that means anyone more than forty-five years old—must realize they put their jobs at risk every time their words or actions make them appear outdated. You will hurt yourself if you regularly make references to the past, lavish praise on popular figures from an earlier generation, are suspicious of new ideas, refuse to abandon outmoded procedures, and are earning a reputation for resisting change.

Of course timeless values endure. An employee will always be measured by his or her integrity, work ethic, performance, dependability, and commitment to the enterprise and its goals. But with every organization straining to be at its very best, you cannot afford to be seen as advocating what has been left behind.

Approach your work with the boundless enthusiasm and creativity of your youngest associates.

ACTIONS I RECOMMEND

1. You will not impress young associates by pretending to be a Hannah Montana fan. You are not their age, and they don't want you to act as though you were. Nor should you offend them by proclaiming that "no entertainer today matches Elvis." Don't make casual comments that date you and cause them to say, "She must be as old as my mother!" Neither they nor your boss want to work with their mothers.

2. Find experts willing to tutor you in the latest digital advances. In doing this book I quickly discovered that pages don't become a book until they are in a Word

Document on a flash drive or on a CD. Once sacred, a printed manuscript is now nothing more than insurance against a computer crash.

This book would have remained an idea if I hadn't found technologically gifted experts who calmed my fears ("Suppose I accidentally *delete* the entire book!") and helped me earn approval from editors who were given a computer instead of a teddy bear when they were toddlers.

Layoffs and a quest for independence have created droves of computer consultants who will make you as competent as your youngest associate. And many are patient and inexpensive (and in the Yellow Pages)! Don't roll your eyes when you see younger associates texting or on Facebook while at lunch. Join them; it's fun and a message to your boss.

3. Many of us find change irritating and complicating. People of every age resist change. Infants become rigid when parents try to slip them into a new car seat. Teenagers refuse to part with running shoes that have become toxic. But while a manager might appease a child, he or she will not tolerate an older employee perceived as slow to accept new policies and procedures; as technology-averse, endlessly complaining that things were simpler in the past; as less physically adept or as rigid in behavior and opinions. Display such behavior and your boss may suggest it's time for you to make way for someone younger.

It is crucial that you frequently assess yourself, asking, "Am I saying or doing anything that depicts me as stuck in the past?" Ask a trusted friend the same question. You might be startled to hear the response: "You keep talking about old movies your coworkers never heard of. One of them asked me if you still go out at night."

4. Even the most compassionate younger authority figure has biases that penalize those considered older. A few months ago I enrolled in a martial arts class to learn a new technique. The sensei—a caring young woman— instructed the class to begin by doing thirty push-ups, adding, "You older students can do fifteen."

   A martial arts class quickly becomes a tight-knit circle in which older students remain outsiders if held to lowered expectations. I told the sensei she made us feel physically limited and that if we did fewer push-ups she and the younger students would hold back in our sparring. Our graduation would be tainted.

   Like the sensei, a manager might assume an older employee will achieve less but is unlikely to say something so politically incorrect. You will find out only when you are brought in to hear that you are not keeping up with coworkers, that you are becoming an outsider in their tightly knit group.

   Never, ever succumb to the temptation to think "I am older and should be excused for doing a little bit less." You will only earn the contempt of your peers and a devastating performance review from your boss. Do the thirty push-ups!

5. I never try to disguise my age and hope you won't either. But I know my entry into any office triggers age-related questions: "Will his ideas be fresh or recycled?" "Will our younger people be comfortable working

with him?" "Is he physically able to spend time on all three shifts, especially after flying to China?" "Does he appreciate how much our industry has changed in the past year?"

I must prove I am the ideal consultant the moment I walk through the door. This requires two very distinct responses from me. First, I must immerse myself in every bit of information that gives me current knowledge of the organization and why it is likely I was asked to come.

Second, early that morning I meditate on the plane or in a quiet corner of my home, letting myself visualize what those in the room want and don't want from me. I will not allow myself to say something that immediately causes them to think "I heard that five years ago." Undertake that same kind of preparation and visualization as you begin a project.

6. Comparisons you and I make must be current. I can't reach back to even the recent past and say "Jack Welch wanted his people to . . ." I don't point to a photograph on an office wall and say, "Oh, Wimbledon; we saw John McEnroe win there." It's not so much that they do the arithmetic ("That's got to be twenty-five years ago!"), but that they begin to doubt the relevance of my advice. They have some interest in my age, but far more in the freshness of my ideas.

You must approach your job in the same way. What does this organization need that only your marriage of experience and problem-solving can provide? The men and women working with you are assessing your ability to bring innovative solutions to current problems.

Your age will cease being a factor if they see your ideas are fresh, even bold. Let them witness your calm in a moment of crisis. "I've seen this before and know how to handle it."

7. Certainly some associates will have heard that you are a grandparent and that you probably began working when they were in elementary school. The way you express these facts will make them strengths—that they see you thriving in the new workplace—or irritating reminders that you prefer memories to actions.

Becoming a grandparent remains cause for celebration in the more traditional companies I go to. But don't expect cake and balloons when you announce your daughter just had a baby if you work for an organization in which only youth is celebrated.

One of the most acclaimed merchants I've ever worked with recently called me, saying, "Bob, Jennie just had the baby; I'm a grandmother!" I rejoiced with her, but I surprised her by advising that she share the news with colleagues who know her daughter but not with the younger buyers. Her reply made it clear I had rained on her parade. She said, "I'm too excited to keep this quiet. I'm telling everyone at tomorrow's storewide meeting."

A few weeks later she told me she had made a mistake. "My peers are almost as excited as I am. But the buyers and junior buyers now treat me differently. Our meetings aren't as lively. Instead of raucous discussions of what's hot and what's not, they hurry through their presentations. They haven't been barging into my office saying, 'You're going to love this dress!' They seem to think I suddenly lost touch with the girls and young women who shop in our stores. I'm no longer the merchant they pleaded to work for. It's as though I've become *their* grandmother."

Make certain you know your audience before saying anything that can cause coworkers to think of you as more suited to an earlier generation. Becoming a grandparent is one of life's great gifts, but it's not in your job description.

8. Lori (and you) must continually demonstrate to your boss that you bring to work a marriage of wisdom and vitality. That unique blend of talents will keep you working until your 401(k) has regained its health.

SOME CLOSING THOUGHTS

The day you start your new job—whether it's your first or fifth—you set in motion events that eventually will bring you into an office to learn your future. I spend much of my time in settings where careers are decided—boardrooms, elegant offices, and cramped corners of a factory or sales floor—and there is a familiar rhythm to the discussions that take place in those rooms.

Before you're called to learn whether you're being promoted, passed over, or perhaps fired, your immediate boss has gathered together those whose opinions will determine your future. He or she begins by describing your performance in terms familiar to every manager: "Is never late with a deliverable." "Is always within budget." "Made our Six Sigma program the best in our industry." "Improved gross margins on a product we had considered discontinuing."

Frequently, those in the room begin nodding their approval, volunteering praise for work you've completed for them. You get the job done, and there is smiling agreement that people enjoy working with you. Given that careers are at stake, such meetings are surprisingly brief. The decision is unanimous, you've won the job. Everyone gets back to work feeling pleased. Your boss calls to tell you the good news.

Too often, however, the rhythm falters and there's a heavier feeling in the room. You've attained, even surpassed, the objectives set for you, but your boss's enthusiasm is muted and comments from others are lukewarm.

One of the participants says, "Look, he doesn't work for me, but I've had problems with him. You can promote him if you want, but he rubs me and my people the wrong way. We'll work with him if we have to."

Once the first stone is thrown others join in, recalling unpleasant encounters they've had with you. In moments blemishes begin appearing on your reputation. Measurable performance hasn't triggered these criticisms, it's how you get the job done, the emotions you arouse in those with whom you work. Suddenly your future is being determined by words like *behavior* and *attitude* instead of *budgets, sales, funds raised,* or *scrap rates.*

The discussion has turned inward, from an objective evaluation of your performance to a personal appraisal of you as a human being. Your attitude, behavior, and character (a kind of intimate ABC) are being laid bare until someone in the room asks—and someone always does—"Would you want to work for him?" The silence in the room has just put your career on hold, or worse.

I've written *What's Stopping Me from Getting Ahead?* for only one purpose: to help guide you past the missteps that damage careers. I don't want you left behind while those of less talent move ahead. I want you to enter that office to hear "Congratulations, you've been promoted!"

INDEX

The main entries in **boldface** are the twelve characteristics that stop employees from getting ahead.

ABOUT THE AUTHOR

Robert W. Goldfarb has been mentoring managers and management teams on five continents for more than thirty years. More than 85 percent of those he has coached continue to win promotions. Prior to starting his own firm, Goldfarb held line and staff positions at AT&T, Mobil Oil Corporation, the Urban Coalition, and Hofstra University. He graduated cum laude and was elected to Phi Beta Kappa at Columbia University and holds an M.A. from New York University. He has written frequently on managing in a changing society.